With Love and Rage

With Love and Rage

A Friendship with Iris Murdoch

David Morgan

KU PRESS
KINGSTON UNIVERSITY PRESS

Kingston University Press Ltd, Kingston University,
Penrhyn Road, Kingston upon Thames
Surrey KT1 2EE

British Library Cataloguing in Publication Data available.

ISBN 978-1-899999-42-2

Set in Palatino
Typeset by: Legend Press Ltd, London
www.legendpress.co.uk

Printed in the UK by Beamreach Printing

Cover designed by Gudrun Jobst
www.yotedesign.com
Cover illustration by Hannah Radenkova

KU
PRESS
KINGSTON UNIVERSITY
PRESS

For Angharad

Acknowledgements

I would like to record special thanks to Dr Anne Rowe and Judith Watts of KUP. I was a first-time author with something to say, but I've chopped and changed and added and subtracted, involving retypes and rereads that would have made most editors despair, but Anne has persevered. I'm not sure what role the shade of Iris Murdoch herself has played, but if a shade can protest she will by calling me an ass for writing about her at all. But seeing me tying myself into knots over it, she may also have appealed to Anne via the ether to be patient and help the poor idiot try to get it right, which Anne has done. What has kept me going, and perhaps kept Anne patient, isn't just reverence for a dead writer, or some imaginary whispery contact with her, or a wish to add to Murdoch scholarship; it is the need to keep her alive in our mind's eye because we loved her or realised we were loved by her. I wrote this to stop her fading for me personally. As she fades still further, other words will be needed, not by Murdoch scholars or by chums reminiscing, but by people like myself who had a more urgent kind of contact with her during a period of trouble in their lives, and who want to keep their particular Iris alive. Such writing is the opposite of scholarly writing; it is a kind of spell to raise the dead where if you get a word wrong the spell doesn't work. Which is why it is so hard. So thank you Anne.

Contents

Introduction

Iris Murdoch and David Morgan met while he was a student at the Royal College of Art in London in the mid-1960s. Murdoch had left St Anne's College at Oxford to teach philosophy in the General Studies Department there. Something 'clicked', Morgan says, and they were to become life-long friends. This frank account of their friendship was written in response to a request for a short essay for the *Iris Murdoch Review* from Peter Conradi, Iris Murdoch's biographer. However, as the 'Proustian floodgates of memory' opened and long-forgotten emotions flooded in, Murdoch's presence became gradually more realised and Morgan's memoir became increasingly more intimate and meditative. What has emerged is one of the more insightful accounts into Murdoch's life and art to have appeared since her death in 1999. As such, it deserves its own centre stage.

This painful, funny and irreverent account of a friendship that lasted more than thirty years vacillates between disrespect and homage, between hilarity and tears and between love and rage on both sides. Morgan describes Murdoch arriving at the RCA 'as a grandee from the world of letters to teach philosophy to a wilder bunch of students than she had ever encountered at Oxford'. But she was more *au fait* with unconventional behaviour than he thought. Her resignation from St Anne's had been instigated by a passionate relationship with a female colleague that had come perilously close to a scandal. At first Murdoch was his moral guide, attempting to sort out the imbroglios of his life, but she became increasingly drawn, quite willingly, off her pedestal and into the sexual mêlée that characterised it. Morgan believes that she relished the intrigue which caused vicarious excitement. The 1960s were precarious times fraught with gossip, innuendo and reputation assassination, and this is both a story of the promiscuous, bohemian London of the decade, and of two remarkable individuals who were part of it. But there is another, more covert, narrative here – about how art is made. For the dark corners of Morgan's life provided the kind of raw material for Murdoch's art that her own background precluded. Some personal compromises were perhaps inevitable and this story illuminates those perilous moral boundaries that must haunt the life of every writer. Murdoch clearly transgressed them, damaging both Morgan and herself in the process, but such transgressions paradoxically enabled the integrity of her art in relation to its truth to human experience.

Born in Birmingham in 1939, David Morgan was sent at 13 to a school for maladjusted children where he 'experienced torments only maladjusted boys can dream up for each other'. He then educated himself by reading library books and attended Stratford Grammar School but left at 16 with no formal qualifications. A nervous breakdown at 17 caused him to be hospitalised against his will in Birmingham, and the horrors he experienced there intrude poignantly into the reminiscences that follow. Believing himself to be only half-educated, he opted to attend Birmingham School of Art to end a vagabond existence and reliance on state handouts. Highly intelligent, he proceeded to the RCA, although his ambition was always to write rather than paint. Peter Conradi gives this account of his meeting Murdoch and their subsequent friendship in *Iris Murdoch: A Life*.

> David Morgan was in his final year as a student of painting during Iris's first, seeing himself a Birmingham rebel

stuck among preciously genteel painter-tutors (apart from the genuinely eccentric Carel Weight and his protégé, the idiosyncratic Pop artist Peter Blake). He had not read Iris's books. As he opened the door of her office with its Goya print, on the top floor of JCR building at 23, Cromwell Rd, for a tutorial in April 1964, they 'recognized' each other – something clicked. She was pleased by the tough way he at once treated her 'as one sovereign state treating with another'. An intense autodidact, he had come through much, including breakdowns, to reach the RCA: she was, after years of secret reading, the first really intelligent person to befriend him, to see and speak to his intellectual hunger. The complications of his private life interested her – she was morally appalled and probably unconsciously excited by his treatment of girlfriends – as by the Dionysiac approach to art he shared with other co-students: a novelist's voyeuristic *frisson* was mixed up with the real help she gave. He saw her as 'feasting with panthers', and her letter referring to the 'paint so enchantingly entangled in [his] hair' links him to Will Boase in *Bruno's Dream*, while the subventions his situation then necessitated prefigure Marcus's to Leo in *The Time of the Angels*. She came to apprehend his dangerous wildness less as something 'charming', increasingly as confused, needing patient understanding. She assured him that their entirely platonic friendship was 'for life'. Over successive decades their meetings dropped, to his chagrin, from three times a year to a mere once-per-year. Iris was the main civilizing influence in his life, sometimes gentle; at other times, when she feared that his 'delinquency', which she partly loved and which he partly acted out as an Iris Murdoch 'character' to keep her interested, might compromise her professional standing, very fierce indeed. She could make 'time stand still'; she could also 'make things happen that only happened when you were with her'. Her admonishing

> but loving letters to him defend precisely that civility which the 1960s threatened, championing privacy, kindness, loyalty, mutual respect. Soon he was a college lecturer living by some of these values: he would tell her how his teaching was going, and she helped him get it right[1].

Morgan's memoir holds a magnifying glass over this, seemingly peripheral, relationship to reveal a clandestine corner of Murdoch's life that few were aware of[2]. This 'record of a friendship' is too unconventional to be called a 'memoir'; it is what Morgan himself prefers to call a 'collage': writing that emulates the actual working of memory in its arbitrary recording of the past as it surfaces in the present. His version of their chaste yet sexually-charged attraction is divided into four sections that follow an opening letter to Peter Conradi, who is the addressee throughout and who acts as both confidant and confessor. The letter is followed by an 'Outline of a Relationship' in which Morgan reveals the intimacy and intrigue that characterised the relationship and attempts to account for Murdoch's fascination with his life. An 'Overview' section describes how he moved 'into the aegis of Iris and how he moved out of it,' and describes their meetings, the obsessional love-life that fuelled Murdoch's interest in him, the near scandal that almost wrecked her career and the gradual infrequency of meetings that finally ceased altogether. The next section, entitled 'I Remember', takes the form of a collage of letters, fragments, conversations, anecdotes and meditations recorded in note form as they are remembered. The notes get increasingly longer and more orchestrated as certain pressing situations invite deeper meditation. Morgan ends with a startlingly honest, if ambivalent, assessment of Murdoch's effect on his life. A letter of response from Peter Conradi, who suggests that Morgan 'captures things [about Iris] no-one else has' closes the collage.

This unconventional structure that relives rather than

recounts the past, allows us to encounter Murdoch in ways that more conventional accounts cannot. We hear her stammering voice; smell her face powder or the moist tweed of her coat in the rain, and feel our own *frisson* at being in that august presence. Morgan's narrative technique unwittingly emulates Murdoch's own in its evoking of another human presence so vividly that she is not merely observed, but re-experienced by readers. As Murdoch metamorphoses from Joan of Arc to Earthy Mangold, from teacher to seductress, from friend to mystic, he brings her alive again. His impressionistic layering of memory alongside a refusal to aestheticize the past results in a startlingly fresh picture of Murdoch – but one often far from flattering. Morgan detected a prurience in her that vicariously 'thrilled' to his sexual exploits and deviances, and a headstrong foolhardiness that teetered on the edge of disaster (predispositions she ascribed to many of her fictional characters). What is unnerving is that his honesty provides at once a fresh sense of closeness to, and a fearful sense of alienation from, a woman who is so different from the one we thought we knew.

What becomes evident is how far Murdoch was entrenched in the times, in the cultural clash between established civilised values and the iconoclasm that characterised the 1960s. Morgan says he would have liked to rock 'the Oxford thing [. . .] to the core' and their mutual fascination was partly generated by difference: between privilege and impecunity; restraint and violence and conformity and anarchy. Morgan's ridicule of Murdoch's 'pomposity' and cut-glass voice, and his increasingly bizarre attempts to shock are part of the social anarchy which characterised a period in history when more young people from less privileged backgrounds had access to higher education than ever before – and perhaps had difficulty in convincing themselves that they were either deserving of it or intellectually up to it. The effects of the 1944 Butler Education Act filtered into contemporary fiction of the period, most notably in novels by Kingsley Amis and plays by John

Osborne. Murdoch was on one occasion aligned with the 'Angry Young Men', though later scholarship was to refute the association. She was disturbed and delighted in equal measure by the bohemianism and wildness, not only of the students but also the staff at the RCA. The sexual *frisson* that underlies her largely chaste relationship with one of those students was perhaps generated, and certainly only made permissible, by that bohemianism. Their relationship began just after the Profumo Affair which had dominated the press since the spring of 1963, and after the publication of *A Severed Head* in 1961, *An Unofficial Rose* in 1962, and *The Unicorn* in 1963, which deal collectively with incest, enchantment, abortion, adultery and same-sex relationships. Embroiling herself in Morgan's life was partly an aspect of Murdoch's own liberation, and partly an attempt to immerse herself in behaviour which she sought to understand and subject to moral questioning in her art. Yet a huge mutual affection transcended both the liberties and confines that the 1960s imposed on their friendship and Murdoch's thirst for vicarious experience: they loved art, literature and words; she was seduced by his charm, touched by his vulnerability, felt for his suffering and encouraged the best in him.

Morgan makes no attempt to camouflage the inconsistencies and contradictions that paradoxically characterise any honest account of the past. He is a typically unreliable narrator, one whose stories sometimes fail to convince and who knows that there are deeply-buried memories stubbornly irretrievable. Such instability demands that we read cautiously – his desire to shock Murdoch then extends to a concomitant desire now to shock 'the shrine makers' who he thinks seek to deify her. He confesses that his 'self' intruded too much into their actual relationship and it intrudes strongly into this remembered one too; we should not forget for a moment that this is a self-portrait as much as it is a portrait of Iris Murdoch. But such inconsistencies, omissions and intrusions are necessary; for this is the wilful and damaged man whom Murdoch loved and whose account of their friendship must be heard in all its frailty if we are to understand its significance to her life and her art. When we laugh at Morgan's egotistic 'seigneurial wave' in restaurants, mourn the tragedy that was his early life and become angry at his irreverent and sometimes shocking disclosures, the love and rage that Murdoch once felt become our own, and are directed at both her and him.

His dissolute love-life, Morgan thinks, was the *raison d'être* of their liaison and believes that Murdoch may have inadvertently intensified his bad behaviour as she engineered the pattern of their relationship and he played to his strengths. She relished his dramas to the point that she became a willing participant who contrived events and affected outcomes. Morgan describes the state he and his lovers were in during the early days of their friendship as 'spellbound' and suggests that Murdoch was equally spellbound, operating inside as well as outside the 'magic circle'. This level of involvement is surprising in itself: in her novels any wilful intrusion into the lives of others is regarded suspiciously and only to be conducted with the utmost caution. She understood that altruism is often infected with self-seeking, yet she was clearly appropriating Morgan's life for her art. In her literary theory, Murdoch fiercely advocates the idea of 'negative capability', insisting that writers should resist the temptation to include either themselves or their personal relationships in their work. Such views imply that Murdoch's novels themselves are wrought out of the imagination, and thus protected as far as possible from her own obsessions and certainly from those of her friends. Yet it is here that one finds an inevitable contradiction in the transforming of the deep loving 'attention' to others that occasions love (which is at the heart of her moral philosophy and clearly evident in her relationship with Morgan), into art. This tension between pure, objective imagination and obsessive fantasy means that the writer lives in perpetual liminality, pivoting on the border of conscious awareness, and on the boundary between an obligation to art that requires her to *see* and tell the truth about the world, and the obligation to one's friends and acquaintances that requires respect for the integrity of those lives observed.[3] 'Other people are, after all,' she says, 'the most interesting features of our world'.[4]

Morgan's strong personality, so powerfully evoked in these pages, suggests itself in a number of Murdoch's fictional characters and allows a rare insight into the creative process itself. The lonely, damaged and isolated outsider haunts her novels, in fact, for decades and, if Morgan is their prototype, he changes gender, crosses class boundaries and can be both thoroughly evil and touchingly vulnerable. But in whatever guise, this figure recurs in novels between the 1960s to the 1980s. Conradi has briefly identified Morgan, via the image of 'the paint so charmingly entangled in [his] hair,' with Will Boase in *Bruno's Dream* (1969) and something of Morgan's violence feeds into her depiction of both the Boase twins. Morgan, however, rejects the idea and recoils from any attempt to identify himself in her characters, though he takes pride in his influence on the detail of her plots. Yet while he acknowledges that there are those who, out of vanity, spot themselves in her characters, he also thinks that there may be those who miss their presence and accepts that he 'may be a case of that'.[5]

Conradi also sees Morgan's relationship with Murdoch echoed in that between the student and teacher Leo Peshkov and Marcus Fisher in *The Time of the Angels* (1966), but this memoir suggests a more intricate web of links between fact and fiction which says much about Murdoch's psychological acuity, provides insights into both her inner life and her narrative techniques (and invites us to think about Morgan afresh too). Leo is 'one of the problems of the age' who wants to 'train' himself in immorality, seeing it as duty in a Godless age and telling lies at every opportunity.[6] But he hides his desire to be better than he is from those who expect him to behave badly. The unquestioning acceptance of his delinquency causes him to construct even more elaborate lies so as not to disappoint. Murdoch understood that such a character plays or acts out immorality rather than living it and her portrait of Leo illustrates her refusal to see human beings as stereotypes. Marcus's feelings for Leo also suggest Murdoch's own misgivings about the wisdom of her friendship with Morgan: 'he had often had small passions for students but had always managed to keep them sealed up. What troubled him here was that Leo so patently knew of his weaknesses' (p.207). A brief comic self-reference demonstrates a sharper understanding of Morgan's irreverent feelings for Murdoch than he himself may have been aware of: Leo says of another 'Murdochian' presence, Anthea Barlow, the middle-aged woman off whom he has been sponging: 'She's so friendly and sympathetic and wants to know about me and help me [. . .], I can't stand her' (p. 134). But direct equations, entertaining and revealing as they are, will only go so far. Ultimately her characters are infinitely complex amalgams: something of Morgan may lie behind Muriel's desire to be a poet and Elizabeth's incarceration and victimisation by a figure of power. The inherent fear of Godlessness articulated by the atheist rector Carel Fisher is Murdoch's own, as are some aspects of the Bishop's demythologised Christianity and the 'do-gooder' Shadox's practicality. None the less, fresh information about Murdoch's life illuminates the extent to which her novels are woven out of philosophical positions, the raw materials of her life and out of the imagination that breaks free from them.[7]

If Morgan does inhabit Murdoch's fiction, then this memoir and the novels together perform a dialogue that casts a loving benign gaze on a man who, like Leo Peshkov, was 'one of the problems of the age'. In the way that Elias Canetti[8] inspired a sequence of enchanter figures, aspects of Morgan's personality are identifiable in another sequence of damaged, outsider figures. Jessica Bird in *The Nice and the Good* (1968) for example who 'had never developed the faculty of colouring and structuring her surroundings into a moral habitation' had a 'craving for the immediate and the ephemeral' that was 'perhaps in the only form in which she could know it, a spiritual hunger'.[9] He is present too in conversations between the young criminal Beautiful Joe and Cato in *Henry and Cato* (1976), when Beautiful Joe reveals his distress at the prospect of Cato's losing interest in him and through fear tries to shock Cato with tales of crime and derogatory comments about women. Morgan's name is compositely present in two of Murdoch's most disturbed and evil characters, Morgan Browne in *A Fairly Honourable Defeat* (1970) and David Crimond in *The Book and The Brotherhood* (1987). But there are benign portraits too: the impecunious art student, Tim Reede, in *Nuns and Soldiers* (1980) is a feckless, but likeable, character. Most striking though is the link between Morgan and Hilary Burde, the damaged narrator of *A Word Child* (1975), whose career and relationships are wrecked partly as a result of his experience in a children's home. Like Morgan, Hilary believes words to be his salvation and when Morgan says that he wanted 'to cut through the intellectualising of the [men] around her, straight to her heart' through the 'currency [of] words', he is searching for the same empowerment through language that Hilary had sought. Morgan thinks the link tenuous, but does say of this book that 'with its guilt-ridden self-tormenting, self-deadening hero, [it] is the only one of her books that makes me blub'.

Morgan prefers to think of Murdoch's characters as formed *a priori*. He suggests they come out of her in the same way that characters came out of Dickens, lifted out, whole. The reason why her art will never completely reveal itself to sober analysis, he thinks, is because so much of it was indeed created at a unconscious level: 'I would argue that when she hits her stride, really gets going, and you can feel her writing fast and easily, she is partly writing from this place. And it is the place – in the case of the great novelist – where her characters live'. While she would argue that art needed to be 'highly wrought,' he would argue that the unconscious mind is capable of wonderful intricacies and structuring, and that perhaps she was using that source more that she thought.

Either way, it is increasingly evident that the novels are more autobiographical than she would have acknowledged or perhaps even recognised herself. Autobiographical fiction, she argues, intensifies the fantasy life of the writer and negates the working of the creative imagination, which is what, for her, defines the greatest art (in Shakespeare, Dostoevsky and Dickens, for example). Admitting autobiographical input would have made both herself and her fiction vulnerable. Yet such disingenuousness is understandable – she wanted readers and critics to focus on moral debates, not facile equations between real and fictional characters or psychoanalytic probing of her unconscious mind. Life-hunting and psychoanalysis she thought were limiting factors in literary theory. She knew anyway that both are identifiable in any art – 'one can only write about the world one understands'[10] she says – and admits that she has 'drawn all these people into a sort of spiral which ultimately is the form of one's own mind'.[11] But these facets of her novels were not where she understood their truths to reside.

Yet the temptation for readers and critics to seek out and sensationalise the autobiographical aspect of novels is seemingly inexhaustible.[12] The shocking element in Morgan's memoir, which is the latest addition to a small industry in biographical interest in Murdoch[13], may well encourage the voyeurism that often accompanies fresh revelations about the private lives of famous writers. Such interest should not damage or diminish the novels, and the challenge for Murdoch scholarship is to find fresh ways of reading her work that can accommodate the extent to which she uses her life in the production of her art. Such understanding will, in turn, enable a better understanding of Murdoch herself, her novels and the mind that shaped them. Autobiography *can* be understood as one of the routes to the truths she wanted to tell in her fiction – those truths about freedom, love, obsession, suffering and God, which can surely only be found in the experiences of one's own life and the recesses of one's own heart, as well as through rational intellectual questioning and attentive, loving observation of others.

Iris Murdoch's friendship with David Morgan is framed by two fumbling farewells, one at the end of their first evening together at Murdoch's flat in Harcourt Terrace in 1964, the second at the station after their last supper at the Bizarro Restaurant in Paddington in the Autumn of 1995. Morgan's reluctance to say goodbye to her then was perhaps informed by a tacit understanding that he would never see her again. This memoir is both a final farewell and a preservation of her for eternity. When he once asked if he could make a life-mask of her from plaster of Paris she refused because she was afraid of not being able to breathe. He has made his life mask now, not of plaster, but words. Writing this memoir was painful and came at considerable personal cost, but his legacy is not just a personal one: it will contribute towards the synthesising of life and art that will one day identify not only what makes Iris Murdoch's art uniquely her own but also illuminate the nature of creative genius.

Anne Rowe
Kingston University

Notes:

1 Peter J. Conradi, *Iris Murdoch: A Life* (London HarperCollins, 1991), pp.475-6.

2 Carolyn Dinan was a student at the RCA from 1964 to 1968. She was taught by Murdoch and says that as such a well-known figure Murdoch was highly respected and her students were in awe of her. She remembers Murdoch's extreme kindness when she took a year out from her studies due to illness, but heard nothing of Murdoch's relationship with Morgan. Though invariably kind to students, Murdoch's affiliations always appeared to be very much with the other philosophy tutors; she was not 'one of us,' Carolyn says.
(Carolyn Dinan in conversation with Anne Rowe, 2 February, 2009.)

3 The soliciting of deeply personal information from many other male friends is, in fact, emerging as a motif in letter runs that have been acquired by the Centre for Iris Murdoch Studies at Kingston University since its inauguration in 2004. In the Murdoch Archives are letter runs from Iris Murdoch to writer Roly Cochrane; the Canadian teacher and scholar, Scott Dunbar and the writer and philosopher, Denis Paul. Murdoch was a prolific letter writer, often spending four hours a day writing them. The complex relationship between her letter-writing persona and her art is explored in more detail in: Anne Rowe, 'Those Lives Observed: The Self and the "Other" in the Letters of Iris Murdoch,' *The Spirit of the Age*, ed. by Meg Jensen and Jane Jordan (Newcastle: Cambridge Scholars Press, 2009), where I also make this point about the tensions between Murdoch's life and her work.

4 Iris Murdoch, 'Art is the Imitation of Nature' in *Existentialists and Mystics: Writings on Philosophy and Fiction*, ed. by Peter Conradi (London: Chatto and Windus, 1997), p. 255.

5 All quotations by David Morgan not taken from the memoir itself are from email correspondence or conversations with Anne Rowe.

6 Iris Murdoch, *The Time of the Angels* (London: Chatto & Windus, 1966), p.74. Subsequent page numbers refer to this edition.

7 For a discussion of the relationship between Murdoch's life and her art see Valerie Purton's introduction to *Iris Murdoch: A Chronology* (London: Palgrave, 2007), pp.x-xix. Purton notes that 'what appears as wild fantasy often turns out to be closely modelled on the Byzantine complexities of Murdoch's emotional life'.

[8] Elias Canetti was the Nobel prize-wining novelist with whom Murdoch had an affair in the 1950s and with whom she remained emotionally involved for many years.

[9] Iris Murdoch, *The Nice and The Good* (1968), p.82.

[10] Iris Murdoch, interview with Glover in Gillian Dooley, ed., *From a Tiny Corner in the House of Fiction: Interviews with Iris Murdoch* (Columbia: University of South Carolina Press, 2003).

[11] Ibid., Iris Murdoch, interview with Frank Kermode, pp.9-13.

[12] The press visited the Murdoch Archives at Kingston University when Murdoch's London Library was acquired by the Centre for Iris Murdoch Studies in 2007. The resulting report focused instead on letters from the Canadian writer and teacher, Roly Cochrane, in an article entitled, 'Murdoch's lust stayed strong despite Alzheimer's'. The *Daily Telegraph*, 1 July, 2007.

[13] David Morgan's memoir is the most recent addition to the cohort of biographical books and essays that has emerged since 1998 when John Bayley's first controversial book *Iris: A Memoir of Iris Murdoch* (London: Duckworth, 1998), appeared before Murdoch's death. *Iris and the Friends* (London: Duckworth, 1999) and *Widower's House* (London: Duckworth, 2001) followed. Peter Conradi's stabilizing official biography *Iris Murdoch: A Life* (London: HarperCollins) also appeared in 2001 and A.N. Wilson's *Iris Murdoch: As I Knew Her* (London: Hutchinson) in 2003. Richard Eyre's film, *Iris*, with Kate Winslet and Judi Dench as the young and old Iris respectively was released in 2002. Nick Turner's 'Saint Iris? Murdoch's place in the Modern Canon' in *Iris Murdoch: A Reassessment* (Harmondsworth: Palgrave, 2006), ed., Anne Rowe, analyzes the effect of this material on Murdoch's reputation. Two short essays by Peter Conradi, 'Iris Murdoch's Pen-Friendships' and 'Divine Though Unfinished: Letters to Roly Cochrane', and Anne Rowe's '"Thou Art the Journey": Letters from Iris Murdoch to Sister Marian at Stanbrook Abbey,' appear in the *Iris Murdoch News Letter*, no.19; Valerie Purton's 'Iris Murdoch and the Art of Dedication' and Anne Rowe's 'I embrace you with my love: Letters from Iris Murdoch to Elias Canetti' appear in the *Iris Murdoch Review*, no. 1, 2008.

The 'Proustian Floodgates' of Memory: David Morgan's Opening Letter to Peter Conradi

Dear Peter,
This began as a long letter to you consisting of one-liners remembered from conversations with IM[1]. I originally planned to record about 30 – the ones that sounded deep or clever or threw some light on her work. But it has ended up as everything I can remember. Here and there I may confuse speech with a quotation from a letter but the line between the two is blurred – something said in a letter is often picked up at a meeting and vice-versa. I kept no record of meetings; she would have been outraged if I had, and letters were sent with the explicit instruction, *destroy all letters* – which of course I didn't – so I have been able to refer to these now and again.

Writing has been stop-start and the text has grown haphazardly. It started as just notes consisting of quotations. But as I added more they got longer and I found myself wanting to tell a story through them – a story of the 60s. But it couldn't be told just by the quotations so I added more and more of a gloss to them which, in the end, became first a running commentary, then bits of narrative in their

[1] Iris Murdoch is referred to mostly as IM throughout. David Morgan's personal notes to the text are indicated with the addition (DM). Other footnotes are editorial comments.

own right needing sections of their own. This drowns out Iris a bit, but there is still plenty of her; and it was the only way I could write it. In some ways I blame you for encouraging me. The act of remembering has opened a Proustian floodgate through which the past has come pouring back, much of it painful but demanding so hard to be recorded that, once I started, I had to go on. Because it began as a letter, I have decided to keep you as addressee even though the text has got so long.

This is not meant to be a critique or mini-biography and the layout is too fragmented for it properly to be called a memoir. What it set out to be is a collage from two angles – the experience of someone loved by Iris Murdoch, and the experience of someone who made her very angry – the Love and Rage referred to in the title. It introduces a fierce as well as a gentle Iris, who is demonstrated in her own words, and the occasional picture it introduces of her in a rage may come as a bit of a shock.

It pulls no punches when it comes to describing either the crimes she ticked me off for, or the complicated forms her love sometimes took. She would have objected strongly to the idea of my writing it because she objected to the intrusion of self into writing, and she would have thought it revealed myself and her in a way that not only exposed us, but also wasn't worth recording in the first place. I have very definitely felt a warning finger being waved … *What bilge; Don't waste time on me Dear Boy; Do a hand's turn for the human race instead.* She might even have been very angry.

Listening to the text as it has unfolded, only one thing has made me uneasy. I'd hoped that the way it rambled would be kept in some sort of shape by the Love Rage theme, but I now see I took this too far. I present myself too starkly as a bad boy and her too starkly as a reformer. This was partly because of that moment of grief you and I shared on Notting Hill just after she died. I could tell that it went deeper with you than it did with me and I thought an account of Iris as a saviour-figure would be what you wanted to hear. But I make myself too contrite, admit too easily to being a case suitable for treatment, and this now strikes me as wimpish and not the way things really were – even though they may have been like it at the beginning. So as the text has developed I have tried to correct this by a change of tone and by presenting Iris herself as less and less of a paragon. I let the neat opposition of the Iris-as-saviour, David-as-being-saved roles become increasingly blurred, and the moral distance between us shorten, until by the end of the piece we have become two people entangled on a more equal footing. This again, is closer to how things were, or at least to how they developed. As my over-simplification of IM's role began to soften at the edge, I began to see her from lots of new angles, some of them surprising, some even outrageous, and some perhaps even imagined. That simple Janus figure that I had started with – Iris loving, Iris angry – split into many Irises: angry, compassionate, chaste, vain, voyeuristic, frightening, comic, silly and finally (heartbreakingly) at the end, even monstrous.

The solecism I was guilty of at all the earlier meetings, when we were still on the pupil/teacher basis, is that *I talked too much.* And I have only realised this in retrospect, when I have been trying to remember what she said about something and it's a blank. If I force my mind back 40 years, I hear her stammering, grave voice saying precious things as well as telling me off. But I also hear my own voice, butting in and talking over hers – pouring its ideas out in a jejune way. Why didn't I shut up? I even – horror of horrors – remember her once snapping at me, *If only you would let me get a word in edgeways*. Anyway – here goes. To give readers some background before they press on to the confusion of the notes, I've added an Outline and Overview.

Outline of a Relationship: Intimacy and Intrigue

During 1964 we met once a week, except in the holidays, and exchanged letters every four days – a frequency fixed by her so she could check that nothing *too disastrous* was happening. When I found the four-day rule hard to keep she said, *Your capacity to not-write letters is about equal, but only just, to my capacity not to receive them*. In 1965 we met once a fortnight, and letters would probably have tailed off too had I just been a *nice boy she had met at the Royal College of Art*. But her interest and compassion were piqued by my increasingly problematic life-style. From trying to help and educate me by sending me books and going round galleries with me, she found herself drawn into my troubles and they clearly kept her interested. All the most interesting things she wrote or said belong to the decade 1964-74, with the most intense phase being the two years 1964-65. Letters from that first year, 1964, contain phrases like:

I love you very much too, (it's odd how one knows these things.) You were sceptical when I first said it but I hope you are less so now.

Clearly I *was* sceptical because re-reading them now I realised with a shock of recognition ... *She* did *love me*. And that many of them were love letters.

By 1974 meetings and letters grew further apart – we met about three times a year, with letters every two months. Between 1974 and 1990 letters became depersonalised to notes of well-wishing, unless I made a big effort and wrote her a really strong letter. This could elicit the old spark and I would get something revealing back. After 1990 meetings reduced to one a year and letters to shorthand notes. E ffectively she had lost interest, and it's no use my softening the blow by telling myself she had forgotten me because of Alzheimer's.

Her 'voice' in letters or in conversation was alternately that of teacher, lover, stern aunt and moral censor, as well as famous author-in-a-rush. Her comments covered nearly everything two people can talk about and I fired questions at her on every subject. There was complete openness on both sides – my openness elicited a similar openness, although apparently she was normally reticent. But although we covered so much ground, what she said fell under two main headings – *exhortations* and *admonishments. Exhortations:* (1) be an artist (2) behave properly (3) educate yourself (4) be of some use to the human race. *Admonishments* came when I was so clearly failing to do any of them. At the time, I scoffed at the idea of an orderly life, but later the penny dropped and I realised that these conversations were my moral education if I'd been prepared to listen to it.

Regarding my voice to her, I can't hear it any more but I can deduce it from her replies. It probably switched between ebullience and muted accounts of suffering. I think it contained a lot of blarney and probably quite a confident pouring out of views – in fact an explosion of them; I'd kept them bottled up so long. A lot of letters and conversations were spent telling her about my latest contretemps *vis-à-vis* people or money, and just adventures generally. I wrote and spoke to hold her attention and to hold onto her, and to have somebody to tell them to. What surprises me on re-

reading her letters are the constant re-assurances:

IM: *Nothing will peter out, and I am not receding.*
You know it's inconceivable I could "finish with you".
I regard you as a permanent fixture. If you can – care for me, and don't fear.
Christ, you should know that you can trust me by now.

A lot of my letters must have expressed worries about how long it would last, and perhaps even contained pleas not to be dropped[2]. When I was in confident mode, there was definitely some sexual blarney. I was dazzled by her in ways I have tried to define, but not sexually. My blarney consisted of writing to her as if we were lovers and it included sexual flattery because I thought this sort of gallantry was called for. I'm sure she saw through it. But there was no blarney about my telling her she was beautiful, or that she was ageless. She was both.

Increasingly, I used her as a confessor to whom I poured out my problems, particularly those centred on my relationship with a girl called Magda. I'd met Magda at a Midland art school. When we both got in to study at London colleges I saw us as twin souls who would take on the art world together. After we arrived I soon realised I wasn't going to make it in that world but she was, and I was going to lose her. So I tried to hang onto her by a combination of bullying and possessiveness – even by trying to mesmerise her. But I was holding her back and she knew she had to end it. She had lost the will to do this by a clean break but dully, mutinously, by a series of small almost sleepy steps, she began to pull herself free.

It was at this point IM came on the scene. It quickened

[2] This should not give the impression that their tone became submissive, or that the pleading was all on my side. She could sound equally insecure. In a letter of Sept. 1964 she wrote, *Yes, you are a wolf, and have sent me a very wolfish letter, full of hostility. You weren't even able to end it affectionately.* (DM)

her interest but blotted out more interesting things we could have talked about. In the end the subject of Magda dominated our meetings. I came to them reeling with misery at the latest instalment of chasing her across England, trying to persuade her to come back to me, and thinking increasingly violent thoughts as other men closed ranks to protect her.

Iris saw me getting stuck deeper and deeper in this mess, which she described as *this magical obsessive relationship*. When she thought the relationship was still saveable, Iris wrote, *I wish I could turn some screw that would make you both perfectly happy*. She told me she had been through the same thing: *I know, I know, about being insanely in love and I have pursued people long and with ingenuity but never with your relentlessness in the face of refusal*. In the end, seeing it couldn't be saved, in letter after letter and conversation after conversation, she tried to snap me out of it and break the spell, counselling civilised behaviour and arguing that Magda must be set free. And even that I would get over it:

I know how one feels that one person can make one at last be oneself, but there has got to be also a central point, even if it is very very small which knows that – without them – it can and has to survive in the face of everything, and be indestructible.

She wrote and said wonderful things – many forgotten – encompassing her views on love, obsession, control and final resignation to loss. Everything she said was good sense, ending with the exhortation to exchange magical power for moral power – like Prospero. When Magda went away for a time, I complicated things by starting a second relationship with Paulette, a fellow painter at the Royal College of Art. When Magda returned I pursued her as hard as ever, and she half came back to me, dragging the three of us into a triangular situation. I try in my notes later to describe in more detail how IM became involved in our triangle – how she was outside it as moral guide, but at the same time inside it as participant. Can I locate her position more exactly? Can I explain why it attracted her in the first place? If I think back and try to see it as she saw it, she would have seen me trying to cast a spell on Magda to get her back, and Paulette trying to cast a spell on me to make me stay. It isn't an exaggeration to use the word 'spell-bound' for the state we were in. She referred to us as if the three of us were asleep, cut off from the rest of the world:

It's time you got out of this dungeon. It seems to an outsider fantastic that you let obsession cage you in such misery.

Don't disappear into some limbo of trouble where even communication breaks down.

And of Magda she said,

She strikes me as someone asleep. I don't think this comatose being is natural to her.

We were too miserably involved – too magically glued together – to realise the three of us made a shape visible to an outsider. If we had read Iris's books we might have realised we looked like one of the complicated tableaux in them, and that was why this strange woman was so interested. But it would never have occurred to us that she might want to join in. She defined her own position in one of her letters, in words that seem to show she was including herself:

No, I don't feel any jealousy here (it would be a sad lookout if I did, I am naturally a jealous person). This is perhaps one thing that the age difference, which you so acutely make me feel, can do for us.

At crisis points in 1965 letters and meetings increased, but in the end she realised I wasn't listening, that her best efforts had failed and I was beyond her power to help. This didn't mean she stopped writing or seeing me. She still kept a watching brief but, resignedly, withdrew a bit, knowing the situation just had to play itself out. Which is slowly what it did, helped by the fact that to hold down a teaching job I had to behave circumspectly. But in the process I became less interesting, and I think this was the real reason that, after about 1969, letters and meetings got further and further apart.

I've decided not to edit anything because I feel the past is too serious to edit – its anguish is too big – and it presses urgently on the present to be known completely. So a lot of trivia is included; only here and there does IM say anything serious or particularly interesting; but occasionally she says something very interesting. Over-glossing what she said rather than just letting her talk may now and again shift the focus too far from her to me. I have typed things as they came into my head; they are not in any order.

What I have written may sit oddly with scholarly articles on IM, not just because it's by a non-academic, but because it sounds like *lèse-majesté*. It assumes a familiarity that verges on cheek, and my interpretation of her motives sounds too knowing. Yet one of the first things she said to me was how much she liked the way I wasn't in awe of her and treated her as *one sovereign state treating with another.* She also flattered me by saying,

I find it hard to communicate with other members of the human race at the best of times but you belong to the small band of people I can really talk to.

This, surely, was more than just the loving blarney she used with people she fell for. As for the glib way I analyse her interest in me and the three other figures in this account, I am on shakier ground. But she herself described people as *endlessly detailed* and strange, coming to everything they do from different directions, with much detail hidden from themselves. Although, she might be a bit huffy about this being applied to herself.

An Overview: First Farewell, Last Farewell

I first met her, as you mention in your biography, in February 1964, in her upstairs office in the Royal College of Art Junior Common Room in Cromwell Road, for a tutorial to discuss my dissertation, which she was overseeing. I was 24; she was 44 and had just published *The Unicorn*. I last met her at the Bizarro Restaurant in Paddington in the autumn of 1995. Following this meeting there was a date at the Stanhope Arms in Gloucester Road, which she never turned up for because Alzheimer's had intervened. Between 1964 and 1995 I met her about twenty times at her flat in Harcourt Terrace, two or three times in restaurants in Soho (Bianchi's and Mario's), and two or three times in the National Gallery (where she tried to convert me to Tiepolo and Fragonard). The rest of the time we met in pubs. These pubs were the Three Greyhounds (Old Compton Street), the Duke of York (Wardour Street), the Swiss Tavern (Old Compton Street), the Hollywood (near Harcourt Terrace) and the Dog and Duck (Bateman Street, Soho). She also came to my room in Ladbroke Grove three times on flying visits.

The only long meeting, the whole evening, was the first one at Harcourt Terrace, where we got to know each other away from the college. She had written me a note asking me to bring some drawings round to show her, and the note had ended, *Be discreet about this.* At this meeting she laid the ground rules for our relationship, which would *not* include sleeping with her but did, that evening, include kissing. Referring to this in a letter the next day, she said, *Perhaps it's surprising that we held out so long with only Piero della Francesca between us like a drawn sword.* So we must have been sitting on her sofa looking at an art book. I can't remember who made the first move – it happened spontaneously.

The evening ended with her coming up behind me and slipping a five-pound note into my jacket pocket because she knew I was hard up, and then she turned me out, in an exalted state, into the rain. The letter following the meeting also wondered whether I was *not by now seeing Wednesday evening as a dream or feeling alarmed and baffled by it.* Not that she expected me to be awed or flattered; in fact she had been pleased, again, by the way I had behaved as if I was her equal. This wasn't quite true; I was in fact very awed by her as a grandee in the world of letters, and excited and disturbed by kissing her. Referring to our ages in a second letter, she reassured me I was not just a young man being 'collected': *You are not, as you observed, all that young and I don't see myself as all that old. You may believe I am 44 but I don't.*

All the other meetings were much shorter – two hours, ending with, *I'm sorry dear boy, but I'll have to kick you out now,* or *Sorry dear boy, but I must dash off.* I don't understand somebody in your book saying the Harcourt Terrace flat was dusty. I never saw dust but I do remember an enormously long sofa – it could hold six people. I remember seeing it as a sign of her gregariousness, and it was fully occupied by a row of people at her party, which I talk about later. It gave no hint of the frightening reserve she was also capable of.

Apart from the first meeting, where I was the 'person of the night', I always got the impression she saw her second echelon friends early in the evening and the real ones later.

Sometimes, I would trail with her in a taxi en route to the higher friend and jump out and vanish just before we got there. One night, the higher friend was Brigid Brophy[3] and we went on foot to her flat before I did my vanishing act. Sometimes, I tagged along with her to Paddington to see her off – usually in the face of protestations. And the last time I saw her, after the Bizarro Restaurant meeting, we ended up with a struggle at Paddington. Perhaps I sensed it was the last time. Anyway, I handed her onto the train then got onto it myself, then off, then on again, clumsily embracing her. It got very physical and confused and she got very flustered; then I jumped off as the train pulled out.

This teetering together – then apart – at the last meeting oddly echoed an incident at the first meeting at Harcourt Terrace, when she turned me out into the rain. My head was swimming with sherry and I had gone fifty yards down the street when, on impulse, I went back and rang her bell. She came downstairs, opened the door and we grabbed each other, clumsily, on the doorstep, pressing faces together, mine streaming wet.

Up to the Wednesday meeting at Harcourt Terrace, letters and meetings had focused on our discovery of each other – the gradual abandonment of formality, even though we were far from being 'those two sovereign states' as she liked to believe, and I was very nervous. However, I rapidly gained in confidence to the point where I became objectionable. Sometimes, in pubs, for example, she would be recognised and I was suddenly in the limelight as her escort. I blush to admit this, but I may even once or twice have given a seigneurial wave to keep admirers at bay.

It came as a surprise, but she wasn't backward about doing this herself. Once, when we were in a pub in Earls Court, a gang of Australians spotted her and asked her if she'd like a drink. A brick wall shot up and she said a very firm 'No thanks', with none of the usual 'gosh' and 'golly' hesitation and courtesy. There was something almost male

[3] Brigid Brophy (1929 – 1995); novelist and pacifist.

about its brusqueness, and almost possessive: an older woman taking on the role of male escort to keep the world at a distance from her and her young man, so that he could pour out his nonsense to her in a corner.

I walked on air when I was with her, in a kind of glow, confirming that despite everything I'd been through in Birmingham – lack of education, maladjusted schools and hospitals – I had been *recognised* by her. But however cocky I got, and despite all her assurances that it was *for life* or that it was *nonsense* that she might drop me, I never felt safe. I sensed that she could turn frosty at any moment, and she had half-warned me of this in a letter – *perhaps it is as well that you should know I can be angry.* Nobody in your biography mentions being scared of her. Am I the only one?[4]

What did she look like – to me? You know from my letters that I found her fierce 'Joan of Arc' look attractive. But I found her body dumpy and, by the time I met her, middle-aged spread had been added to her natural stockiness as a girl. Ungallantly therefore, when she made her ground rules at Harcourt Terrace (*You won't be able to go to bed with me*) I was at first surprised that it had been brought up at all, then relieved. I was also surprised in A.N.W.'s book[5] that he thought of going to bed with her – how did he *dare*?

What did she wear? She did *not* always wear a shapeless mac as some accounts have it. She could vary from aristocratic bag lady to female Cossack with trousers and tunics. My usual impression was of trailing voluminous tweed coats that could have been from Oxfam, but weren't. She rolled when she walked, almost stomped, legs encased in thick lisle stockings, as – yes – Joan of Arc (her again) might

[4] According to Conradi, A. S. Byatt was 'frightened' at their first meeting, and was still alarmed 25 years later. He describes others being scared of her: Norway's best-known war-hero, Max Manus (DSO. MC and Bar for mining German warships in Oslo harbour) recounted that he found sitting next to Iris at dinner frightening: 'she looks so hard, and gives away so little' (Peter Conradi, *Iris Murdoch: A Life* , 2001), p.515. Referred to hereafter as *IMAL*.

[5] A.N. Wilson, author of Iris Murdoch: As I Knew Her (2003).

have stomped.

But the Joan of Arc of Denis Healey and other men friends was *their* image of the young Iris, based on the 1928 film[6]. My Iris was still Joan, but one who had aged a bit and stomped her way back to the mud and the beasts. The page-boy haircut had turned into a more ragged helmet, and the head that carried it was bigger and heavier, and the body sturdier. She was still a radiant and valiant Joan, but a more weather-beaten one, whose raptures had turned into a peasant woman's bouts of absent-mindedness.

My truest impression, and I say this with tenderness, was a combination of Joan with a figure who had haunted my childhood – Earthy Mangold, the sister of the Children's Hour scarecrow, Wurzel Gummidge. They had the same pudding-basin hair, the same old coat flapping in the wind, and both braved the elements. I think the picture of a dotty but fiercely intellectual Earthy is the closest I can get, if you can imagine an Earthy in whose head rolled Plato, but in whose dottiness were signs of the dottiness to come. What this leaves out is the warmth that also rolled from this figure, its radiance. It also leaves out the sensation when I first met her *that I knew her.* I had encountered this figure before.

Her feet puzzled me. She had hammer toes (you mention them). I couldn't believe they had been caused by trying to wear, through vanity, daintier shoes than her feet were made for, so thought perhaps her parents had tried to economise when she was a child by making her go on wearing shoes she'd grown out of. But would they have done this to such a loved child? Or were they the result of sharing shoes with Philippa Foot at Seaforth[7], Philippa's feet being smaller?

[6]*The Passion of Joan of Arc* (1928) starring Maria Falconetti as Joan of Arc.

[7]Refers to the flat at 5 Seaforth Place which Murdoch shared with the philosopher and fellow Somervillian, Phillipa Foot, in wartime London.

One was always the first to arrive when one met IM. One would see her stamping her way towards one, coat flapping, face sternly focused. If we were meeting at a restaurant, she would always have said, *Go in and wait for me,* but I was too embarrassed to do so, so would wait outside for her. Once inside, she would pick a table carefully so that I saw her against the light, and this would sometimes involve a bit of re-seating to get me away from her deaf side. This shifting achieved two things: it let her watch everything that was going on and – deliberately or not? – softened her face so that I saw it in a sort of rosy haze. Her face, though stern, became rosier and hazier the more I had to drink, and it was certainly *not* 'innocent of face powder' as A.N.W. says. She would have taken her coat off and I (pray god my manners stretched this far) would have helped her off with it to reveal, in the earlier meetings, a white silk blouse with cherries on it. As the evening progressed the blouse became more luminous and the cherries began to swim.

It was the first time I had been to restaurants and my attitude was a combination of awe, acute embarrassment and sniggering. Once in Bianchi's, for example, I laughed hysterically when the waiter set fire to a dish. I had heard of flambéing but it was the first time I had seen it in action. We have already compared notes on how impossible it was to pay for anything. She was very much in charge and did all the ordering. It was even impossible to pay for a drink in a pub. I tried this once and she considered it for a moment then decided against it. This got me into the habit of being paid for and it was exciting, particularly as she had said sex and money were linked. Being paid for was also a delicious luxury when one was on a grant, still facing a series of summers on the dole. It went to my head and the habit of always being paid for got me into the habit, later on, of begging.

I was surprised by your saying, 'She liked a jar'. I got the impression she liked pubs, but she never drank much with me – at the most we had two glasses of very dry sherry each, which I would get from the bar having been given the money. This would be enough to get me drunk, but she stayed sober. I can only assume she did more serious drinking with the higher friends later in the evening. I was very jealous of this set, whoever they were, and piqued that, despite all her attention, I was always dropped at eight or eight-thirty for them. I was to meet them and learn some of their names at her party (described later), but it was not until I read your book that I realised how strictly she kept people apart. Who else she saw in London was a mystery. When we met she had always rushed *from* somebody to me, or was rushing *to* somebody from me. Her trips to London from Oxford were a frantic round of seeing people, and she whisked from place to place by taxi. I remember, for example, telling her I had a secret to show her in Brompton cemetery, and before I knew it, she had got us there by taxi and we were gazing at the secret – an enormous bell I had discovered in a crypt there, apropos the novel[8]. This bell is still there forty years later, and you can glimpse it through the grille.

To get back to Iris and drink – two snippets: I remember, at a seminar at Cromwell Road, being surprised to see her with a hangover. Her face was puffy, her eyes were bleary and she was chain-smoking to get through it – the aftermath, I thought jealously, of a night with the real friends. The second is a casual remark in one of her letters about *a place in the Harrow Road which I used to frequent for the cheapest strong drink in London, when I was younger*. I live near the Harrow Road and it would be interesting to pinpoint this place, if it still exists. It seems a remote place to buy drink, and outside her stamping grounds.

She always addressed me as *Dear Boy* or *My Child*, which I found affected. But my heart melted when I re-read some of her letters and saw that several of them were signed, *Look after yourself, dear unwise child.* She also called me *wolf boy, darling boy, and wolfling,* and a cheque arrived once with a

[8] Brompton cemetery features in Murdoch's novel *Bruno's Dream* (1969).

note, *I enclose something to keep the bank manager away from the wolf's door.* In one letter she wondered whether I was, in fact, a werewolf. She cosseted me by letter, worrying about hiccups and flu and my being forced to eat parsnips for a week! This tone was to change.

I never detected an Irish accent, even when she told me she had one:

I have an Irish accent you could cut with a knife even though it may have Oxford overtones. It's odd that you just hear my mother's accent but not mine. Our voices are so alike.

Why couldn't I hear it? Her mother, whom I met in her Baron's Court flat in Comeragh Road, had a strong Dublin accent, and their voices were not alike.

To some extent you misconstrue our relationship, or I mis-described it. I don't see myself as Will Boase in *Bruno's Dream*. I know I described myself as a delinquent and her letters to me seem to confirm this. What her letters also show, as well as all the blarney about *paint so charmingly entangled in my hair* etc., is that she recognised my intelligence and my suffering. When we met, in 1964, I didn't interest her as a badly-behaved pretty-boy. I had written a good thesis on oratory and its power to sway crowds, unwittingly covering some of the same ground as Canetti's *Crowds and Power*, a book she recommended. She said of my thesis that it went some way to *proposing a new theory of language*. Admittedly, this was in a testimonial, and we all know how she over-praised her friends, but it wasn't quite the kind of thing Will would have come up with.

When I met Iris, the hopeless pursuit of Magda had knocked the stuffing out of me. I couldn't concentrate at college and was doing increasingly silly things. It was only by an act of will, and with IM's help, that I could go on living, finish my thesis and put up some sort of painting show. My debt to her is that she spotted my intelligence, gave me the confidence to face the world because she had chosen to know me, and – although in the end she thought her best efforts had been wasted – partly civilised me. But as writing has progressed I have had the temerity to see her as a wise woman capable of intrigue, rage and a voyeurism that went beyond just the curiosity of a novelist. This voyeurism didn't just involve me and my relationships; it was seen in her wider flirtation with the RCA. She got embroiled with a crowd who excited and shocked her. And even though their wildness became increasingly a cause for worry, she crossed a line and let herself be drawn into the action. In my case, she reacted compassionately to the triangle I found myself in and the suffering of the people in it, and did her best to unravel the mess. But rather than staying outside as a counsellor, she jumped in as described and joined us as a fourth person; *You stuffed up Paulette with stories about my attachment to you. Magda came to see me in college because you had been telling her friend I was deeply in love with you.* And the degree to which she was *physically* as well as emotionally involved was demonstrated at an RCA Diploma Show where Paulette pulled her hair (which I describe later). She would never have admitted this and would have justified it – as she did to me – by saying, *You dragged me in; You sought to involve me.*

One evening she invited Magda on her own, to Harcourt Terrace, ostensibly to hear her side of things and decide how she should step in – on my side, to help me get her back, or on her side, to make me set her free. I had gone on about Magda at such length, and so obsessively, that IM may have built her up in her mind's eye into a magical being who just had to be viewed. I had certainly said that she was very beautiful.

In fact, I'd gone on about Magda to IM, and on about IM to her (probably deliberately), creating a sense of competition between them and making them curious to meet. I think IM invited her and she went so that they could get a look at each other. IM wasn't really meeting Magda as somebody she wanted to help or for a Murdochian encounter with a magical being. She arranged the evening to meet a rival she was dying to see. So to that extent she can be said to have dragged herself in.

They had two meetings I learnt about only later. I never knew what they talked about except that IM reported that she had asked if Iris thought I was mad.

DM: (on tenterhooks) What did you say?
IM: *That you were perfectly sane.*

The worst thing Iris accused me of was dragging her into was the Keith affair, and this involved no vicarious thrills. It was horrible for everybody involved. I haven't been able to face it squarely. It was the most painful moment of our relationship and almost ended it and, as she said, could have led to her resigning.

Keith was a pale rain-coated boy. Like many RCA students, including myself, he had left school at 16 only half-educated and gone to art school. My case was different in that art school was a last resort to end a vagabond existence. My education had already been wrecked at 13 by my being sent to a school for maladjusted boys, and again at 17 by a nervous breakdown and hospitalisation in Birmingham. But for Keith and the rest it was a legitimate educational move to go to art school at 16 and not do A-levels. The talented, like Keith, could end up at the RCA or the Slade. Most took this route because they were 'good at art' and not academic. But a few, like Keith and I, knew we'd missed something and tried to educate ourselves in an *ad hoc* way by indiscriminate reading. Like a lot of autodidacts we mispronounced words, were bursting with facts and argued without knowing how to. We sometimes listened to ourselves and admitted it didn't sound right. We also pitted our wits against each other in endless games of chess.

A state of one-upmanship existed between us, almost a competition to see who was least illiterate. This was a contest I felt I had won when I heard him pronounce 'skeleton' as 'skellington' and when he received letters in painfully joined-up writing from his mother, which I used to compare with the flair of my own mother's writing when letters came from her. On the other hand, he was a better painter and always beat me at chess. It also ignores the fact that I myself referred confidently to a play called 'Go-eth's Forst' (Goethe's 'Faust') and that my father was subscribing to a 'Masterpieces of Modern Art' part-work featuring a painter he called 'Monette'.

General Studies at the RCA, and the gang of Oxford academics brought in to teach it, spoke to our needs but we also worried that they would see through us the moment we opened our mouths. His high intelligence and mine each needed to be recognised. Mine to some extent had been by the beginning of my relationship with IM, but perhaps he felt his had not. The situation was tricky because letters in a third kind of writing arrived, this time in a flowing blue hand and it was obvious who they were from. I never waved them in his face but I remember dashing off notes back in the same style, which could well have irritated him.

IM had seen that problems could arise. She was worried that I would leave letters lying around and he would read them: '*I trust you but not your flat.*' But she may also have predicted that things could go wrong in other ways and urged me to get a *poste-restante* address. Things came to a head when it was time to submit our theses and hang our final shows. One night, Keith was being fatalistic about what grade he'd get for his essay. I don't know what possessed me, but I said – as a flip remark – that 'with my connections he would be OK'. In an even more flip way, I added something about Iris being charmed by working-class boys, rather pointedly leaving out the 'us'. With some justification he immediately singled himself out as a working-class boy being patronised and threatened not to submit his thesis and/or hang his work, which would have failed him his ARCA (Associate of the Royal College of Art). In a panic I confessed to IM, knowing it would end the relationship, and was duly lambasted in a letter which ended it or, at least, ended it as it had been.

She was frantic with worry. She wrote to Keith and he wrote back, giving her his side of the story. She even made a special trip from Oxford to see him, and I felt a stab of jealousy when in one of the flurry of letters between us about the affair, she used the word 'child' for him (her word for me):

I cannot live with myself if this child is lost.

According to her, he claimed that I had told him she had patronised his looks, his accent and even his thesis subject, and she in turn accused me of deliberately poisoning his mind against her over a period of months:

God knows what other lies you have told him about what I am supposed to have said.

Had I said any of these things? Being accused so fiercely of saying them by both of them, my conviction that I *hadn't* began to waver, but I was more than half convinced that I hadn't. She certainly believed I had.

Before this business she had said:

I do recognise you as somebody who could be a deliberate wrecker of something you value, but I am not afraid of this here. Perhaps I imagine I can manage you and *I care for you a great deal and that will have to stand whatever shocks there are. I'm not that easily jolted.*

But she *was* jolted, and now she said:

You have an instinct for estranging people you are fond of. I suggest you enjoyed using your power to hurt Keith and using him in turn to torment me. I'm afraid this can't be overlooked or got round, and you have destroyed an innocent and happy affec - tion I had for you. I have always been very careful as a teacher. But clearly the worst and most foolish thing I ever did was to make friends with you. I'm not going to abandon you (unless you so wish it), but we must make another start on a different basis. I know I have a responsibility for this disastrous friendship. I stand by my mistakes. But you are a very dangerous person to have for a friend and it would be irresponsible of me to go on as before.

Looking back, I don't think Keith's threats would have been carried out; but I was in a fright about him failing. I also calculated that I'd better get in there with a confession before Iris found out anyway. This horrible affair ended by her damning me to him as a self-aggrandiser (true) and letting him know she'd given me hell, with the net result that the thesis was submitted, the paintings hung and Keith got his ARCA. Surprisingly, the affair even seemed to bring us together. Because she had bustled round so hard on his behalf and believed his side of things, he felt vindicated and, more importantly, *included.* From now on I couldn't lay sole claim to her – he had been drawn into a threesome. We were now in a sense both 'IM's boys' – boys who by now looked white and drawn by the enormity of what they had put her through, but were oddly, because of this, on better terms.

I gave up trying to explain my side to IM. She gradually came round and eventually said, *I am no longer concerned with who said what or to whom.* She told me my punishment would be five years before things got back on the old footing but we were, in fact, on writing and meeting terms again within a year. However, the old intimacy had gone. She had once told me, *If you are patient I will tell you everything about myself,* and she had told me a lot. But now I knew I would never hear the rest. I waited the five years, hoping she would open up in the old way, but she never did.

Over subsequent years we went on seeing each other in

the scaled-down way described – every couple of months – then two or three times a year – then once a year until 1995. Even now, in an emergency, she would make a special effort to see me.

I resigned myself to the new terms and was glad to get what I could. I knew that my original friendship with her – in that all-out heady year of 1964, which could have gone on being other heady years – was one of the most important things I had ever thrown away. I also knew that I had had a sort of excuse which she recognised – the pathological *instinct to estrange.* But IM's rules were IM's rules – a third party had been hurt, or pretended to be hurt, and she was remorseless. How I ever got her to open up so much in the first place now amazes me. I thought at the time that she was that open with everybody. I never knew that the tiniest pressure would make her snap shut.

I don't mean to say that she shut-up completely. The fact that the remembrances that follow cover so many years show she went on telling me things. But what had gone was the rush of complete intimacy where she poured things out the way she and John Bayley[9] had poured things out to each other all night at the start of their relationship. From now on, everything she said was weighed first.

Something else happened and later notes look at this in some detail. Slowly the balance of power changed, and how this happened is dealt with more fully there. To some extent I lost my awe of the Iris Murdoch of the early 1960s, and it wasn't just out of exasperation at her not revealing herself. She became less a sibyl, less a *grande dame.* I began to find her flustered and sometimes a bit doddery, and I mean well before Alzheimer's symptoms. I don't know whether anybody else noticed this; it merged so well with her slightly stammering gravitas that you could easily miss it. The article by Dr Peter Garrard in the first edition of the *Iris Murdoch Review,* where he describes how the beginnings of the destructive process of Alzheimer's always predate the

[9] John Bayley, Murdoch's husband, referred to occasionally as JB.

onset of intellectual difficulty by years, even decades, may explain this[10].

Without wishing to make the 'Overview' too heavy with detail, or pre-empt later notes, a description of our last meeting may be useful here in conveying a picture of the *marginally* failing Iris, when one suspected, but couldn't be sure, something was wrong.

Everything about lunch at the Bizarro was sad and somehow askew. She sat against the light as usual but for some reason had chosen a table in the middle of the room where we felt exposed. We were both tongue-tied and the meeting was one that I had begged rather than been offered. The food arrived. She had ordered Parma ham and it came in dark, red, wafer-thin rashers that I chewed and couldn't swallow. It was so elastic, so impenetrable, that in the end I looked across to see how she was getting on with hers and saw that she was chewing hard with a slight air of consternation, which she was trying to hide. So we munched in unison trying to get through it. The whole thing was miserable. The name of the restaurant felt wrong (surely it was a garbling of 'Pizarro' the Spanish conquistador); we were sitting in the wrong position; she had ordered the wrong thing; and I could see she was beginning to worry about her train. We were now well into that phase of the relationship where I had begun to find her muddled and distant, and her face in silhouette seemed to emphasise an act of self-cancellation that was taking place – a sort of humble opposite of the way she had sat against the light in the old days, in order to be attractive. It was almost apologetic, and as I watched her struggling with her ham I felt a wave of the feelings I had had for her in the old days. She only came alive briefly at the end, with a flash of the old Iris, when I tried to pay and she said she would scream if I didn't shut up.

10 See Peter Garrard, 'The Iris Murdoch Text Analysis Project and its Importance to the Study of Authorship and Alzheimer's Disease' (The *Iris Murdoch Review*, 1: 2008), pp. 14-18. Referred to later as *IMR*.

She paid, and we walked the hundred yards down Praed Street to Paddington Station with me carrying her case. She was ahead of me and I have tried to remember exactly how she walked. She was plodding with slightly longer steps than usual, intent on getting her train, and I even had the impression she was trying to shake me off. We turned left down the slope into the station and found her platform. The train was in – a short four-coach affair with a name like the Oxford 'Hopper' and the doors of the compartments were open. She got in and the strange mixed-up goodbye with me getting on and off the train began.

When she died in February 1999, I felt a sense of loss; but not the void you felt. This was because letters and meetings had dwindled and, though I felt she was still there wishing me well, I also felt she had moved on and I was now on the fringe of her enormous circle of friends. I reasoned that as I had normalised my life I had, at the same time, become less interesting. Vanity and a reluctance to believe she could have had frivolous reasons for knowing me (like fancying me) stopped me facing what was probably also true – that I was older and less attractive. I didn't know whether she had forgotten me or just felt that my troubles were 'sorted'. Equally, she may have felt that *I* had withdrawn and that, by settling down with Paulette and having a daughter (which I did in 1975), I had taken myself out of play. Whatever the explanation, I felt abandoned and, to avoid being hurt, took a tough stance and blanked her out.

I have tried, both in the background and the remembrances that follow, to describe in detail how I moved under the aegis of Iris, and how I moved out of it. With such an extraordinary woman it was an approach to a *presence* and then a withdrawal from it, and you measured it in degrees which you remembered. A lot of people talk about encounters with her but hardly anybody talks about the protracted, and often agonisingly small, steps, over a period of years, by which she said goodbye. Or – to put more bluntly – what it felt like to be dropped by her.

It felt pretty awful. Like Anna Quentin, IM was too decent to go in for bit-by-bit tactics when it came to accustoming people to her infidelity – 'deadening the sharpness of jealousy by a series of little shocks until in the end the victim became resigned to the liberal scope of her affections[11].' She did it by keeping them so far apart they didn't know enough about each other to get jealous.

When it came to being dropped you did suffer rejection by degrees in a way that wasn't calculated, but if you were at all paranoid could feel as though it was. In fact, you just belonged to a crowd of people who had been so over-collected that it was impossible for her to spend as much time on you as she once did, because she had moved on to others.

You dreaded each letter being a shade more formal than the one before it and tried to work out what scale she was using in order to know how long you'd got. When, for example, *Dear darling wolf boy, very worried about your hiccups* (1965) was scaled down to *Dear Boy – in a rush – hope all's well* (1985), I knew I was in trouble. But on a day-to-day basis this fractional cooling wasn't visible and you could kid yourself it wasn't happening.

And you did have several assurances. One was that having been collected in the first place she didn't want to let you go, and she tried terribly hard to convince herself, and you, that it wouldn't happen or wasn't happening: *Nothing is getting less, dear absurd Morgan.* Another was that it was happening so slowly you had plenty of time. And a third was that nothing you did would make it end suddenly. There would be cooling periods and turning points and the relationship might be put on a new footing,

11 This description of the character Anna Quentin – arguably a self-portrait by Murdoch – comes in *Under the Net* (1954). The actual quotation reads, 'deadening, by small and steady shocks, the sharpness of jealousy, until in the end the victim became resigned to the liberal scope of her affections' (*Under the Net*, 1954; London: Vintage, 2002), p.33. Later references refer to this edition.

as in the Keith affair, but once she loved you she was un-driveable away. And I tested her as probably no-one else had ever tested her in this direction.

You weren't so daft you expected to be loved full-strength for more than a limited time, but even Iris Murdoch's love scaled-down was more than worth it. What was the length of her love-attention span? Her *full* attention span? She seemed to be able to love somebody all-out for about a year before her 'emotional promiscuity' kicked in and she fell for somebody else. In the case of John Bayley, it appears to have been for life. In my case it was about a year or a year and a half (1964-5). For the next ten years I managed to prolong it by my troubles and my suffering, and perhaps by providing vicarious excitement and yelling if I felt things slipping. I may have got longer than most.

I miss her much more now, nearly ten years after her death. What I am really doing in these notes is trying to invoke her for myself – to see her staggering affectionately towards me again – and it almost works. But there is no 'almost' about her voice – it is as clear as if I was listening to a recording. It is only now, coinciding with a new period of uncertainty in my life, that I feel the hole she has left.

I Remember: Notes on a Developing Friendship

A collage of letter fragments, conversations, anecdotes and meditations

Anything and Everything (1)

IRA – Bombing the Post Office Tower (1971) IM: *The scum – it was my favourite building in London.*

Sleep – IM: *I crash to sleep like falling into the ocean.*

Tell me – IM: *I am sure I only told you that to lure you into telling me things: Was it like that – or that – or that? I love being told things.*

Virginity – IM: *I couldn't wait to get rid of it.* But didn't say when/whom.

Boasting – IM: *I flatter myself I write rather good prose…When I am the subject of PhDs…*

Defeatism – DM: 'I wish I could turn life off.'
IM: *The tap's on, my boy.*

Cartoons

She often bought newspapers but ignored the news and went straight to the back to the cartoons. I remember Billy the Bee, Charlie Brown (but not Modesty Blaise) and TinTin. I didn't think of her as an innocent that early in the relationship; I was still too in awe, so the cartoons were a surprise. I could try to be clever by saying she liked them because they were platonically 'simple', but that's just being clever. She responded to them at a much more basic level, the way she responded to dogs, to Trabb's Boy in Dickens and, when she was in her seventies, to the Teletubbies on TV. She even muttered their names affectionately. I was surprised, though, that so many of the cartoons appeared in right-wing papers. The revelation of her as innocent – as in some ways naïve – was as much of a surprise as my recognition of her later on as the opposite of innocent, which is dealt with and perhaps overstated later.

Pursuit and Pursuers

(Apropos my chasing Magda):
IM: *I have also been relentlessly pursued and I have hated the pursuer. Then, when I wearied him out, I felt sorry.*

She was an expert on pursuit and gave the impression that she was always the one who was pursued. But I see from Anne Rowe's article on IM's letters to Canetti in the *Iris Murdoch Review* that she pursued him as hard, and for as long, as I pursued Magda, even into the early years of her marriage[12]. When she told me I'd got to let Magda go she spoke as the champion of everybody being chased, determined to stand up for their rights and keep at bay the shadowy obsessives who were after them. Now, forty years later, it is touching to see she was chasing somebody as hard

12 See Anne Rowe, '"I embrace you with my love": Letters from Iris Murdoch to Elias Canetti,' *IMR*, pp. 37-41.

as I was. If the dating of her letters between 1962 and 1975 to Canetti is right – showing her persistence and his evasiveness – she was still pursuing him in 1964 when we met. The heart-rending letter of 1965 *shouted – your windows dark – tried again 8.30* echoes my own trips across London, shouting at blacked-out windows, at the same time. I used her to pour out the misery of my situation. She betrayed no sign of her own misery and had no-one to pour it out to. What I also detect is that by 1965 Canetti had had enough and – like Magda in my case – had begun to batten down the hatches against her for good.

By an extraordinary coincidence I see that one of the letters of 1965 from Steeple Aston invites him to a party at Harcourt Terrace at 5.30pm on June 9th. By checking dates I see this is the same party that I gate-crashed with my RCA chums and which I describe later in these notes. How agog she must have been for him to turn up, doubting in her heart he would. Now I ask myself – did he in fact come? I am getting *déjà vus* of a troll-like man who looked taller sitting down, a troll with an acid tongue and a shock of wiry hair who sat as if enthroned. But if he was there, why wasn't he mentioned in her letter the next day identifying who people were?

Dazed

She took as firm a stand against promiscuity as she did against chasing.

IM: *I disapprove of promiscuity. It is so often connected with being not oneself but in a daze.*

She spoke as somebody very much herself, and not in a daze, delivering a Murdochian judgement. But as with her prohibition about pursuing people, she seemed blindly and touchingly innocent of the fact that she was deeply involved in both herself.

A.N. Wilson: 'she was emotionally all over the place.'[13]
Anna Quentin: (paraphrased) She was bound so closely to so many people that she was forced into one long act of disloyalty in order not to hurt them.[14]

Cats at Night

Caterwauling on rooftops at midnight in Comeragh Road, near her mother's flat.

IM: *They sound like souls in torment.*

This was one of those time-standing-still moments I mentioned; it was a frosty night and one almost literally saw damned figures crouching with their knees to their chins on the roof tiles.

Rene[15]/Alzheimer's

I met her mother once. IM took me along in tow. I don't know whether she was showing me off or not. I don't think so. It was the night we heard the caterwauling.

Because I still had my *grande dame* image of Iris I expected her mother to be grand too. I remember a rather confused old Irishwoman with white hair, nice but not grand. I almost expected to hear her refer to her as 'our Iris'. Seeing them both together, I completely understand her bewildered, 'Now how did I give birth to *that*?'[16]

The point of this note is that through the seventies I knew

[13] Quoting Rachel Trickett, see *IMAL*, p. 282.

[14] The actual quotation reads, 'her existence is one long act of disloyalty; and when I knew her she was constantly involved in secrecy and lying in order to conceal from her friends the fact that she was so closely bound to all the others' (*Under the Net*, p.33).

[15] Rene Murdoch, Iris Murdoch's mother.

[16] This remark conveys her astonishment at the changeling she had produced. (DM)

her mother had Alzheimer's and was waiting for the blow to fall on Iris. But I can't remember how I knew; it was a hunch – an amateur diagnosis. I certainly didn't get it from Iris; she didn't put a name to what was wrong with her. It was all lumped together as dementia then anyway, or old people just being 'difficult'; so she wasn't afraid for herself. Did Rene Murdoch have Alzheimer's? No biography mentions it. But the mother/daughter hereditary link confirms it for me.

God Zones

The only person she ever introduced me to (apart from her mother and very briefly David Hicks[17]) was Father Gerard Irvine, the priest of Saint Cuthbert's in Philbeach Gardens not far from Harcourt Terrace. It was a hot day and we went there on foot. The church had a rear door, shaded with laurels, in a back street. This more mysterious door was the one we went in by. Inside, light shone dimly through Victorian stained glass and there was the faint smell of incense you get in High Anglican churches, that always smells 'wrong', somehow illicit.

Father Irvine met us in his cassock. What was said isn't important; the fact that it was a church isn't important. What is important is what led up to it. I saw IM doing something completely ordinary – going to see somebody – approaching their domain – going in – meeting them. But it was so startling that I can vouch for the fact that the scenes in her books where a character approaches the domain of another – goes into their god-zone – isn't just the application of her formula. I saw with my own eyes that when she herself met people she went through the same excitement as her characters. She bristled with expectation at the moment of meeting;

[17] David Hicks was an Oxford contemporary of Murdoch to whom she was briefly engaged. Conradi describes him as 'good looking, saturnine, talented, penniless, very attractive [. . .] [with] the reputation of a Don Juan' (*IMA L*, p. 203).

a shiver ran through her. It was almost as if a bell tolled as she entered their presence. And because I was with her, I felt it too. I'm not saying anything dramatic happened: my hair didn't stand on end, but my scalp tingled.

I can only compare it to an experience somebody once had with Thomas Hardy. He and Hardy were walking on the downs and suddenly the impossible happened – a flock of birds rose out of the ground in front of them. The birds had been nestling in a dip, but Hardy's companion felt that he had seen them only because he was with Hardy.

Laughing

IM: *You laugh like a devil. I shall miss your devil's laugh.*[18]

I was pleased at laughing like a devil. I thought I just *laughed.* But now I was being told it sounded like something out of Milton. I guessed it had always sounded a bit sarcastic but now I began to hear it – Miltonically – as a sort of squawk of contempt for everything. I had been 'Iris Murdoched' into a devil.

You Could Say or Do Anything

There was one way she was different from everyone else you knew. You felt that whatever you did, it would be OK. With everybody else we hold back. But with her, you had the assurance you could completely let go. You could do anything. You could stand on your head, grow horns, gnash your teeth, talk filth, turn into a monster in front of her and evacuate from every orifice – and she would understand! She might give you a telling-off (and my God did she tell me off!) but would never abandon you. She might even just burst out laughing.

I wouldn't call her maternal, but in this respect she was

[18] She assumed I would go back to Birmingham after the RCA and referred sadly to it. (DM)

like a mother – the only other figure we dare do this with. The trouble was that as with a mother, you were driven to test her to the limit to prove to yourself over and over again that you were safe. The next, and a later note deal with efforts to shock. The first was just misbehaviour but the second was an attack on what I saw as the whole Murdoch crowd and its civility. Perhaps even the Keith affair was also a sort of test – 'after *this* can you still love me?'

Misbehaviour at Her Party – 5.30 pm June 9th 1965

I turned up at Harcourt Terrace with a gang of chums from the RCA (they were uninvited). Not amused, she said pointedly, *David, you can see to **your** party over there*. The party went to my head and I compensated for shyness by extrovert behaviour. I sneered at a quiet woman in mannish clothes for liking A.E. Housman's poetry, and was contemptuous of the 'sapphic' angle she saw in it. And I was amused by 'Mrs Moncrieff', a sort of female old buffer who was a bit out of her depth. Sensing bad behaviour about to happen, IM came and stood next to us to shut me up if I went too far. Looking back, could Mrs Moncrieff have been related to Proust's translator? The mannish woman was Esmé Langley, editor of England's first lesbian magazine. Also present were L.P. Hartley the novelist, Father Gerard Irvine, Christopher Cornford (RCA Dean) and Professor John Wisdom from the London School of Economics, a philosopher and psychologist who was beginning to cast an interested eye in my direction. Stephen Spender was supposed to be coming and I whined a couple of times about him not turning up. I was bursting with a mixture of snobbery at being in the same room with these people, and shyness verging on terror. I also felt I had to fulfil a role as protégé and *enfant terrible*. Things came to a head when I somersaulted over the back of IM's sofa, without spilling my gin and tonic. Later it burnt a ring in the varnish of a table that had to be re-polished and she complained about in a letter the next day. She also complained that somebody in 'my party' stole a bottle of whiskey. She drank Teachers, as you know. In retrospect – and it has just occurred to me with fresh horror – I seem to remember somebody had given her a special bottle, like 'the' Glenlivit, but with the label customised with an italic pen in Gothic letters to read 'the Iris Murdoch' whisky. Was it this someone in my party stole?

After the Party[19]

There were two vague figures at the party – Canetti, who may or may not have been there and on reflection probably wasn't, and Magda who, I now realise, quite definitely was. Probably because I had been showing off and making a fool of myself, she and I quarrelled and began to make a scene and Iris, who had been on the lookout for trouble, stepped between us. I was drunk and tried to push her away, but the push turned into a punch and I hit her quite hard in the left breast. I hit Iris Murdoch. It was an accident but the blow landed and I can even remember the thump of my fist on her white silk blouse and the solid Irish body underneath. I was too far gone to be shocked by what I had done and she certainly wasn't shocked. I had the impression that her body, unlike other people's, wasn't affronted by being hit, that it would remain everkindly no matter how many blows I landed on the white blouse. I'm pretty sure it was the first time anybody had hit her. But despite this 'innocence' she seemed to understand that by doing it I had put our bodies into a sort of complicity, and part of this complicity of bodies was that

[19] This memory surfaced later, perhaps because it had been suppressed, not because of anything awful I did, but because of something Iris did, or that I thought she was doing. It should be read therefore as a sort of dreamlike footnote to the party, at a slightly fuzzy distance from it. (DM)

they sometimes traded blows – and this excited her.

Remembering her role as hostess, she just said sharply, but kindly, *'Not here David – later'*. I have thought a lot about what she meant by the word, *later*. It was a mysterious word to use at that moment and I am almost certainly misinterpreting it. But it was as if she was saying, *Not here – this violence – among my friends – these civilised people – but afterwards ... perhaps violence will be permitted.*

This is so untypical of what one would expect her to say, knowing how she hated violence, that I could almost believe I had dreamt it. The only proof that it happened and that she said it is a letter that I wrote to my Mother describing the party, which I kept a copy of but have now lost. But if it did happen, and I'm sure it did, and if it meant what I thought it meant, it shows Iris's deepest moment of entanglement and most mysterious moment of ambivalence in all her dealings with me.

I heard it as a veiled invitation to stay behind and continue where I had left off when the guests had gone. Then Iris would throw off her disguise as literary hostess and moral guide, a second self she had been hiding all evening would emerge, and she and I and Magda could be our selves. Until this moment, I had only ever felt her wanting to join in. But now the word *'later'* seemed to be promising, even threatening, suggesting that the moment had come when she was actually going to.

Later could mean anything, and how Iris might join in was equally unclear, but whatever it was it was going to be pretty exciting. I tried, drunkenly, to predict what it might be. Was she going to reveal herself to me as Circe and change us all into pigs? Or were we going to shed our skins and dance round the room in some other shape? Or could it mean that the two of us were going to continue our row with Iris as referee under a different, and more abandoned set of rules from those that had been in force when her guests were there?

What rubbish this must sound to those who have already

been offended by the alternative Iris I am presenting. Commonsense and the distance of forty years tell me that all she was saying – all *later* meant – was that she wanted us to stay behind so she could act as peacemaker. I am the first to testify that she was one of those rare people whose first instinct when they see anybody in trouble is to put things right. And she tried to put my troubles right over and over again, so much so that I can even begin to doubt the other picture I have presented. If I could fantasise that picture when I was drunk at her party, could I have been imagining it all those other times as well? But drunk or not, I don't think I imagined it. Nor did I imagine it in the past. Drunkenness probably made me misconstrue exactly what she intended by that word at the party, but not the tone of voice used to say it. And the tone of voice promised the breaking of all rules by a wilder Iris Murdoch than many of her admirers dream of.

The party wound down and one by one the guests left. I hung around. At the very least, *later* seemed to guarantee that I could stay after they had gone, whether or not something else was going to happen. Magda was still there, still sufficiently in awe of the evening to have stayed behind as well. What happened next, when the three of us were alone in the room, is a blank. I have racked my brains to get at whatever it was that I have suppressed. I have looked for and can't find my scribbled note. Did we undergo a transformation – link hands in a wild reptilian dance, slapping our tails on the carpet, being ourselves at last? Or did she just calm us down and then say, *Bedtime my dears, I'll have to kick you both out.*

Two Rooms

Before throwing a crowd of people together in her room and trying to show her in such a complicated way as a ring-mistress of their antics, perhaps I should have described the room in more detail. The room before the party, with just the two of us meeting there, was a much chaster place. It was the place where we had little snacks, sat with art books, sipped whisky, broke the ice and were gradually so overwhelmed by each other that we kissed. Somewhere along the line, my apprehension of her room changed; it stopped being chaste and became, in my imagination at least, the scene for orgies. What changed it? Perhaps there had been some hint of a difference in her behaviour – the faintest taste in the way she kissed me of something lascivious...just the movement of a tongue perhaps (and probably imagined). But it made me rethink who she was, what she was, and why I was really there.[20] This second Iris, erotic and complicated though still massively wise and loving, made her first full appearance at the party and is increasingly the woman described in the second half of these notes. But before starting to deal with that figure, I need to go back to the more innocent history of the room.

Eating Chez Moi

She called her flat *'chez moi'* which impressed me, although the Frenchification irritated. I had one lunch *chez moi*. It consisted of Garibaldis (*I wonder why they're called Garibaldis?*), triangles of fish paste sandwich and a Penguin each, plus Teachers – a perfectly nice little picnic meal. I never went to Cornwall Gardens because I was never invited. Descriptions of its squalor and horrible food remain a spectre. I may have sometimes been drunk at Harcourt Terrace and seen it in a blur, but never so drunk I would have missed the mess people describe at

[20] I am not the only man to have been disturbed by kissing Iris. Writer and journalist Peter Conrad (not to be confused with Peter Conradi) wrote – in an article entitled 'Who Really Knew Iris?' (published in *The Observer*, Sunday 16th September 2001) – 'The way our teeth clashed when she gave me a kiss and the darting, adder-like sorties of her tongue between my lips [...] How do you reconcile the wise omniscience of her mind with flirtatious waywardness of her body?'

Cornwall Gardens. I got the impression John Bayley didn't go there.

The Lavatory and the Sofa

I was always too high, too in awe and too nervous to go to the lavatory at Harcourt Terrace. Nor did she – was she also shy? I was also too embarrassed to go in a pub or restaurant, though she stomped off to the Ladies a couple of times. I remember, once, in a restaurant, she disappeared into the Ladies for ages and came back having washed her face and combed her hair. Her hair was plastered down and I think she had put fresh powder on – somebody who normally had no truck with beauty, girding herself to face her young man and the world. But in her flat a certain squeamishness reigned, a concentration on higher things. She never went to the bathroom or the bedroom, and only very occasionally into a small kitchen – everything happened in the living room.

The living room was filled by the sofa. When one was drunk and a bit in awe the room became the HQ of a Muse, its six-seater sofa the platform where her public sat. And she came out of the kitchen like a sibyl to her public – in my case a public of one. The thrill of the first meeting was that the sibyl actually sat down next to me. She even referred to a '*drawn sword*' between us. A drawn sword that would stop us sleeping together but wouldn't stop us touching.

By later meetings the sofa reverted to its role as just a sofa. I suppose she had bought it because it would hold a lot of people. She hated mislaying anybody – she liked a full house. And the things that happened between us on the sofa became more normal. At the second meeting we

The point, in his case and mine, isn't whether she was kissing us sexually or not, it's that she was able to make us fantasise that she was; and it played even more to male fantasy by the way it contrasted so wickedly with her frostiness. (DM)

sat with the 'sword' on our laps again, but it had stopped being a sword and gone back to just being an art book on Piero. We touched and kissed occasionally after that, and she made that comment about skin being *wonderful stuff*, but in the end we often just sat side by side looking at books, with no more than the occasional sharp intake of breath.

Teeth

The first meeting had been a mixture of feelings – excitement that a famous novelist was interested in me (even seemed to fancy me) – awe at her physical presence – apprehension about what it might entail physically – drunkenness – and last of all, and most confusingly, a moment of revulsion when I kissed her. I had been used to kissing girls at the RCA, and must have kissed her too hard, because she pulled back and said sharply, *Careful*. I worked out from this that she must have had dentures and was afraid that I might dislodge them.

Smells

I pooh-pooh a lot of the descriptions of the mess the Bayleys lived in. I saw no mess at the London end. But smell, the most evocative sense, might bring her back. Can I remember the smell of Iris Murdoch? I remember the smell of gabardine in the rain and the smell of moist tweed from an overcoat, also the smell of face-powder when I gave her goodbye pecks. But I never smelt anything unpleasant except once when we were sitting on the sofa and I caught a whiff of monthly female odour. As a menstruaphobe (made-up word) I gagged slightly at this, but found myself making the fascinating observation that at forty-four she could still have children. I'd always assumed she was post-menopause. It also seems to contradict John Bayley's assertion that she was past childbearing when she married him at thirty-six.[21] Having gynaecological thoughts about her was disturbing.

A Sharper Note Creeps In

IM: *I don't propose to offer you flattering pictures of yourself. I may offer unflattering ones.*

And by contrast with the *paint so enchantingly entangled …* tone at the start of the relationship, she subsequently made quite nasty remarks about me being lazy and vain. Because they were unpleasant, I've blanked them out, but they were along the lines of … *blah, blah, blah, your very handsome self* … or *if you could stir your good-looking* … etc.

IM: *Why don't you do a hand's turn for the human race? Why should I support you in literary idleness? When I am working hard in Oxford you are swanning off round the Isle of Skye.*

I got the rough side of her tongue when it came to job-hunting. She made long-suffering attempts to help me get a teaching job or get to university (about which she was dubious). Even here there was comedy – such as our encounter with a mountebank who would train me to teach English to foreign students for ten pounds. I remember once how she exploded when I got wrong the name of a chap I had asked her to write to, and she posted off a testimonial with a grotesquely garbled version of his name.

IM: *I've had enough of your tomfool behaviour – in future make your own arrangements.*

[21] A.N.W in *Iris Murdoch as I Knew Her* (2003), quotes John Bayley as saying, 'Thank God, when we got married, Iris was past childbearing age.' A.N.W adds in brackets ('she was thirty-six'), (p.15). (DM)

Unshockable
DM: I may do things that will shock you.
IM: *You could surprise me but not shock me.*

As I grew bolder I tried to shock her – not just as an *enfant terrible* but to dent the patrician thing which I resented – and sadistically (even sexually, I now realise) to dominate her as a woman. I also felt that I had a special relationship with horrors. When other boys had been studying for their GCEs, I had been sent to the school for maladjusted boys. When other boys were going to university, I had been instead through the experience of Ward 10, Rubery Hill Hospital, Birmingham. I thought this gave me the right to give this effete crowd, including IM, a dose of the real world.

I had, in fact, had some fairly extreme experiences. At thirteen I had shut myself in my room, where I read and masturbated and refused to go to school. This was treated with seven months in the maladjusted school where I experienced the torments that only disturbed children could dream up for each other, and tried to continue my education by going to Stratford Grammar School in the daytime. But this was only a taster for being properly locked up at seventeen-and-a-half (after another session of seclusion and intensive reading in my bedroom) in the Birmingham hospital. Here I witnessed the raving of lunatics in a proper old-fashioned English mad-house. I saw this as picturesque rather than terrible, but what frightened me every day was that I might be given electric-shock treatment against my will (I wasn't). I thought it would brain-damage me and blank out all the facts I'd been piling up since I was ten. I'm not going to appeal for sympathy – as I did with IM – by pretending it all began as a case of being misunderstood or mixed-up. That I was a sensitive boy shutting himself away from the blundering philistines in his own family to do all that reading. In fact, I was dangerously unhappy and reclusive, at loggerheads with everybody I came in contact with, and couldn't continue living at home, so had to be sent somewhere. Twice.

I told IM some of this and there were gruesome things to tell: for example, boys jumping to their deaths from fire-escapes at the maladjusted school. And – at the hospital – patients being strait-jacketed, cadavers being plugged, maniacs with bells or trailing chains attached to their clothes, but worst of all was the continual screaming from the women's side. And, of course, the fact of being locked up. I played these things up a bit but was, genuinely, still shell-shocked by them. She sympathised, but had heard worse.

So I jumped forward in time to when I had been discharged and led a tramp-like existence in Birmingham, before getting into Birmingham School of Art.[22] I felt intensely lonely and cut off. The smoky streets of the city echoed the smoky wards of the hospital and late at night the derelicts hanging round the Bull Ring could have been patients allowed to roam. I ended up there night after night. Convinced I would now be on my own for good, with no chance of a girlfriend, I decided to throw my lot in with them. They weren't so far gone they weren't still looking for some kind of sex, and one night I let one of them pick me up and follow me across Birmingham to my digs. I described this to Iris, painting a sordid picture of what happened when we got there – our shabby, drooping underpants and the shabby bed. At the prospect of sex about to happen, I felt her interest quickening, but I halted the account, too embarrassed to continue. She wanted to know what happened next ... *And then,* she said, *And then – what?*

And then in an almost sadistically down-to-earth way,

[22] I got in through a piece of farce rather than an effort to reinvent myself. I drew my left foot in biro, took this single sheet of paper as my portfolio through the streets of Birmingham to the art school and was accepted on the spot. Anybody could get into art school in the 1960s; they were another kind of 'asylum' for thousands of misfits and

prompting me to the final confession ------ *He RAPED you*! In fact, he hadn't; it had been much more pathetic and mutual; I couldn't supply the climax she wanted and just mumbled something non-committal.

I could see the account had interested her more than anything I had told her so far, but once again it hadn't shocked her. Nor was she shocked by bloodthirsty tales about what I would like to do to men involved in the saga with Magda. Her response to these was simply, *Come off it David.* I remember her commenting on my attempts to shock her sexually: *'I think I have experienced everything, but that is not the same as knowing everything. I am very puritan, and also a woman.'* I did manage to shock her, though a year later and in the last way I would have wanted, with the Keith affair.

The Writing Machine Rolls on Regardless

I thought of her as a great novelist writing deathless prose. I also thought she took my troubles home with her to Oxford, and I was genuinely concerned in case worrying about me interrupted the writing of a novel, making me responsible down the ages for a misplaced adjective, a half completed sentence ... I taxed her with this:

DM: 'Look, there isn't a danger that my troubles could ever, you know, when you're writing…worrying about me…'
IM – *Uhuhh?* Then slowly getting my drift, *That's very thoughtful of you – I can see why you might think – It's very sweet of you but no – err – it's OK.*

I realised I needn't have worried. My troubles in London hadn't got a hope in hell of putting her off her stride.

oddballs and interesting people, talented and untalented, but in all of whom the life-force ran strong, and this partly explains the wildness of the RCA crowd that so excited IM. (DM)

Casualty Chums

I've already divided her friends into first and second class, the first class being people she had known all her life: writers, politicians, grandees, old lovers, ex-Oxonians and the second people she had picked up more recently. I've also described how each was allocated a different half of the evening, the first class friends getting the more important second half, after 8pm, when she could drink and let her hair down. But one could identify another small and unique set of people – the 'casualty chums': people with a problem she was dealing with and who, if it was an emergency, might be seen any time. It is the casualty chums who think most kindly of her now.

I was a casualty chum. A feature of being a casualty chum was that you knew she was worrying about you and this kept you going. Some casualty chums, like me, exaggerated to themselves how much she was worrying and imagined, as I did, that one's trouble filled her horizon and would quite definitely be taken back to Oxford. The most self-centred, and again I was one, even thought it might occupy her thoughts when she was writing. It came as shock to realise it didn't.

The Shrine-Makers

There is another category of chums which has emerged since her death. I would call them the shrine-makers. Who are the shrine-makers? They are the people, many of them misfits, many of them spiritually adrift, attracted to her because they have been looking for some sort of logos all their lives and find it in her and her books. Your great metaphor that sees her as Piero's 'Madonna della Misericordia' spreading her cloak to shelter a crowd describes what she was and is to these chums. She is their Goddess of Wisdom, their Rule Maker, their Moral Guide. And their devotional circles have gone the next step and perpetuated her in an IM industry, not as cashing in but as something frailer – the need (extending your metaphor) still to ride through life on her skirts.

She was nobody's Madonna. She offered practical help to scores of people but she wasn't as self-abnegating as they think. She stoutly declared to A.N. Wilson, for example, that she deserved the Booker Prize; she boasted to me about one day being the subject of PhDs; she approached the Gifford Lectures like a woman rolling up her sleeves to do battle and she would have wanted her books read after her death. But she would have indignantly dismissed the over-reverence of this weaker sort of admirer – for their own good. I think her wisdom would have taken the form with them that it took with me and come as a demand that they stop mooning about, sort themselves out, see to the people in their lives and, if necessary, forget her. Although she would probably have said it a bit more kindly than she did to me.... *Come off it, you asses.*

Quibbling Over Words

DM: 'I don't agree with your use of the word 'descry,' it's archaic.'
IM: *It's a perfectly good word.*

I note that others have also tackled her about archaisms, even made-up words: for example, 'oblivescence' in *A Word Child.*

DM – 'I don't understand why you describe light as "grains". (I was thinking of *Under the Net* where "the darkness was coming, in a granulation of deeper and deeper blues" and "the darkness hung in the air but spread out in a suspended powder".)[23] In all your novels, when light is changing like a blue sky darkening, you talk about light as grains or powder. To me – and surely everybody – light is

[23] *Under the Net*, p.106 and p.212.

smooth. Your descriptions of evening light in London and Paris are wonderful but then you bring in these grains and suddenly I stop seeing it.' She stuck up for grains as firmly as she'd stuck up for 'descry', but I saw it as a failure to be true to her senses. I wasn't convinced she'd ever seen light as powder.

DM Criticises (again!)

Having already criticised 'descry' and 'grains', I went on to complain about a lack of what I called 'concretising' in some of her novels:

DM: 'When I read, for example, about a character sinking in a marsh, the words should make me *sink* with the character. You and your writer friends may slag off Kipling for his jingoism and lack of intellect, but for me his prose has precisely this power to plunge me into what he describes. I am *there*. For me, in *The Unicorn,* the marsh your character sinks in is just a notional marsh – he isn't really sinking. Your marsh remains the *idea* of a marsh. Could being a philosopher be stopping you being a good writer?'

(I read in your *Life* that Ivy Compton-Burnett said that IM would have been a better writer if she'd trained as a Norland Nanny instead of doing philosophy.)

IM: *You're quite right. Effingham was never really sinking in that bog – it was all intellectual. I've got a novel coming out in the autumn where somebody is burnt to death, but they aren't real flames.*[24] *The answer is not Joyceisation or Millerisation, but some kind of courage.*

Writing/Writer's Block/Post-Novel Tristesse

IM: *To set about the business of writing some deliberation is*

[24] Probably *The Italian Girl* (1964).

necessary; at some point a form must be chosen and one must find the optimum method for pouring out what one feels within into something that has strong independent being without. More of this another time…

IM: *…it's a question of getting drive and technique together. I've got plenty of both but they don't co-ordinate properly – it's misery.*

IM: (she described a writer friend of hers who was 'blocked')
DM: What can a blocked writer do?
IM: *I think this is one of the most important problems – and one where nerve and courage count (a sort of belief like Peter walking on the water.)*

IM: *I have already finished the Irish novel and feel a bit odd. These things recede and disappear so rapidly when they are done – and the characters one has lived with so closely all go, like people emigrating, quite suddenly – one feels positively lonely.*

Keeping it a Secret

IM: *I never divulge details of a novel while I am writing it.*

I don't think she went so far as to see novel-writing as a pact she mustn't break with the Muse. But she did see it as a craft that had to be practised in secret and then unveiled. She was also naturally a secretive woman, and I mention her admiration for 'secretive' writers like T.E. Lawrence. Keeping it secret was a serious matter, and she gave the impression that if she gave anything away it would 'blow' the novel. She told me about the character burning to death because the book was about to be published, but never anything in mid-write.

Obscene Letters

IM: *I'm always depressed when a novel is published because it drives home my failure to do anything first-rate, and I get a batch of unpleasant (often obscene) letters as well as nice ones.*

Mums

IM: *Deep down all women are mums.*

It was a surprise to hear her come out with something so corny. She said it as a practical tip for me regarding my lover and I sneered at it at the time, thinking of her – naïvely – as a higher being who wouldn't do anything as boring as follow the behavioural formulas for her sex.

Indira

DM: (after Mrs Gandhi's assault on the Golden Temple at Amritsar) 'Is she Kali?'
IM: *Of course not, I had pillow fights with her in the dorm at Badminton.*

(I know you dispute this because they only just overlapped and Indira was older.[25] But she definitely said it, and I don't see why an older girl shouldn't have larked with a younger one.)

The Mythical General

She told me that the Commander in Chief of UK forces in the Falklands was a cousin of hers – a General *Westmoreland* or *Richardson*, I can't remember which. It was said with authority, as a factual aside, and I had no reason not to believe it. But reading that she had a cousin, General

[25] Indira Gandhi was at Badminton School from July 1936 to March 1937; her mother had died early in 1936.

Alexander Richardson, Royal Ulster Rifles, I now wonder if she fancifully shifted him from World War 2 to the modern conflict.

You were the first to say I should take some of the things she told me with a pinch of salt. At first it seemed like the most awful insult, and it confused me that you were as much in awe of her absolute integrity as I was, yet at the same time seemed to be saying ... 'Well you know, the old girl came out with the occasional whopper which we lovingly forgive'. I couldn't then – and still can't – connect Iris Murdoch with whoppers– the occasional bit of romancing on her dust-jackets maybe, but no more than that.[26] I remain baffled by the truth or fiction of pillow fights with Mrs Gandhi, driving ambulances in World War 2, and now this mysterious General. I still don't dismiss the idea that they could all be completely true.

What One Wore to Meet Her

In the early days, I dressed 'art-studenty' in paint-spattered clothes. This wasn't because I'd taken her reference to '*paint so charmingly entangled* ...' as a cue; all I had at the time were old clothes. When I started teaching I dressed better, and might even have worn aftershave. I needn't have bothered because I remember her saying, *You needn't dress up for me*. I may even have looked too smart because I remember her making the occasional acid remark about *Your very hand - some self*.

She could certainly cut people down to size when she wanted to, or was I the only one she did this to? I remember other disparaging remarks about my 'smart' phase.

[26] In 1996 Murdoch claimed, not for the first time, to have been engaged to Frank Thompson, which she emphatically never was. The question might be put: not whether she told untruths, which she probably never knowingly did, but whether she came, like many novelists, to *believe* untruths that suited her mythologising.

She referred to cuff-links she'd bought me from Harrods as my *lapiz-lazuli earring's* and when I met her while wearing a silver signet-ring I'd bought myself on the Portobello Road, she said tartly, *I'm glad to see you've made it legal* (it was on my wedding finger). But the most cutting put-down wasn't to do with the way I dressed. It came in response to a letter I wrote her under the influence of LSD, not in my normal voice, but in a sort of echoic God-voice AS God. It prompted the sharp reply, *Dear David, thankyou for your letter and impersonation of God. I have met another higher incarnation since, rather more convincing. Can we meet on Monday?*

Morgan's *Chez Moi*

Having described going to her, I need to describe her coming to me. It was disturbing to have Iris appear in one's room. She came three times, twice on surprise visits. The second was when my father died; the first was early in the relationship and I suppose it was to see how I lived. 129 Ladbroke Grove was a typical student pit of the 1960s, almost empty apart from a few broken sticks of furniture from the Portobello Road. It was as squalid as these places were, with the added nastiness of a floor I'd painted in bitumen that had never dried, so it squelched underfoot. And it had two unusual features. In one corner of the room stood a lean-to built by an earlier flatmate out of clothes-horses, blankets and the odd plank, to give himself a bit of privacy. In effect, it was a small house, but I had never bothered to dismantle it.

A second disturbing feature was a row of milk-bottles against one wall, full of urine, their necks plugged with plasticine – a relic of lazy nights when I couldn't be bothered to go down two floors to the shared lavatory. Anyway, the door opened and Iris was standing there. She looked round the room – at the floor shining with tar, at the lean-to made of blankets and at the bottles of piss and didn't bat an eyelid. Her *sang-froid*, faced with my room, makes me wonder whether those accounts of her and John Bayley's mess are in fact not exaggerated – she *found the room completely normal.* Her only criticism – more an interior-design tip than a criticism – was that she thought I needed, *a few decent bits of furniture.* Then, her eye was caught by some papers on my table, and the atmosphere changed. She became very interested.

Love Bites and Lists

The first thing she picked up was a sheet of paper with a list of names. She scanned it approvingly, thinking it was the raw material for a poem. Then she saw her own name. The list was in fact some sort of silly male tally of the women I had known. By her name I had written, 'She love-bites like a horse'. I thought she would have a fit, but all she said was, *Oh – I love-bite like a horse do I?* and seemed not displeased. In a letter afterwards she wrote, *and don't put me into lists. I deserve paragraphs and poems to myself.*

The Brief Wechsel

The second thing she picked up was a bundle of her letters neatly stacked alongside some of mine to her. This time she pounced, and said nastily, '*Oh – you're keeping a 'brief wechsel' are you*?' I had to look this up in a dictionary when she'd gone – and found that it was German for preserving both sides of a correspondence. It was horribly embarrassing; she was very nasty indeed about it and it disturbed her so much she referred to it several times in letters. It is why, in one letter, she says, *another for your collection.*

Blabbermouth

IM: *You're a blabbermouth.*

I knew the ever-kindly Iris that you and John Bayley describe but as I have said she could also be withering. She could make remarks that flattened one. This remark referred of course to my role in the Keith affair, which still makes me go hot and cold. She had a passion for secrecy, perhaps not only forced on her by having to manage her huge group of friends and lovers without hurting them, but also for its own sake. When I read about her arranging secret ringing codes with Canetti[27] and empty-envelope messages to Steeple Aston, and how she left letters in hollow trees in the War, I remember my impression at the start of our relationship that she was trying to OVER-hush me about it – *keep your mouth shut; tear up all letters* – over and over again. I also remembered how attached she was to 'secretive' writers like T. E. Lawrence, who played things close to their chests, and for whom intrigue was perhaps part of the creative process.

Dogs

You know how she adored them. If there was a dog in a restaurant where we were eating, she would be distracted. I'd be keen to show off and engage in deep talk, but the fascination of the dog was stronger and she would interrupt me in full flow by turning her gaze to it. I think she put dogs on a pedestal – saw them as bodhisattvas.

Eavesdropping

Again, in restaurants, I would be trying to tell her my latest ideas about Shakespeare or Dickens, but she would be distracted by other diners. This contradicts the many references in your *Life* to each person she spoke to feeling they

[27] The writer, Elias Canetti (1905-94), winner of the Nobel Prize for Literature in 1981. Murdoch had an affair with Canetti between 1953 and 1956 but she remained emotionally attached to him and they corresponded for many years.

were the focus of attention. She eavesdropped almost as a caricature of the novelist getting 'copy' – agog to everybody round her.

Smoking

IM and I both puffed nervously on cigarettes at our meetings. I remember these in a haze – a haze of smoke, drink, and dim lighting. I could get quite high on this. To an impressionable 24-year-old, particularly a self-educated, intellectual snob of 24, this combination of half-light, fug, and drink, and the interest lavished on me by a middle-aged famous novelist, was seriously heady stuff. But at one meeting an ingredient had changed – the magic smoke of our meetings was missing. Between one meeting and the next she had given up smoking. I lit up and began to puff and she snapped:

IM: *I see you're still smoking those drug sticks.*

The Box from Blackwell's

She told me there were big gaps in my education and that she was going to fill them. One day my education arrived at Ladbroke Grove. It was a large rectangular parcel with a 'Blackwells, Oxford' label on the side. Before I read the label, I thought for a wild moment it might have been from Fortnum and Masons. It contained *The London Shakespeare* (green cloth, in six volumes), Donne's *Complete Poems*, Hardy's *Complete Poems, The Tale of Genji* by Lady Murasaki, and *Njals's Saga*. Each had a compliments slip inside. No Dostoievski, no Henry James and no philosophy. I realised the books weren't in fact my education but her own favourites. I read and re-read *Njals's Saga*, opened Hardy once, then not again.

T. E. Lawrence

We discussed writers a lot, along the lines of my saying, 'Is X a good writer?'... 'Why is X a good writer?' We had our differences here.

DM: 'Is T. E. Lawrence a good writer?'

(Personally I found him a pretty bad writer with a grandiose, constructed style, as phoney in its opposite way as his masquerade as Airman Shaw. She wasn't having this.)

IM: *You've got to realise that he was part of a secret generation.* (She may have said *secretive.*)

What I saw as posing, she saw as an interesting kind of *hiding*. I could see she admired Lawrence deeply. She said in a letter, *I have a lot to say about T.E. Lawrence and D.H. Lawrence,* but never said it.

Dickens

(1) (I know I've told you this before but you seemed to miss how spot-on it is. Perhaps this was because it is unexpected, whereas for me it, at last, explained Dickens.)

DM: 'Is Dickens a good writer?'
IM: *Yes, of course he is, but he is a criminal.*

I remember, when she said this, being shocked. Then saying to myself... 'My God – she's right...this is more like it...this is what I've been waiting for – *one word* that cuts through all the crap and is closer to the mark than pages of literary criticism'. Incidentally, I got the impression that although we were almost as mutually in awe of Dickens as of Shakespeare, Shakespeare's 'invisibility' made him a 'cleaner' and therefore greater writer – not embroiled with himself like poor Dickens. We disagreed here.

(2) IM: *Even a character who appears for a few seconds can stick in your mind for ever – like Trabb's Boy.*

She spoke as if she actually *loved* this character, as if simplicity spoke to simplicity,

Waugh

DM: 'Is Evelyn Waugh a good writer?'
IM: *Second-rate, lightweight. Don't waste your time on people like Waugh, read the classics.*

I disagreed. I thought Waugh had bite and am pleased to see John Bayley thought *A Handful of Dust* was a good novel. I was surprised that, in one of her letters, she said, *No – I don't know who John Beaver is, I rarely read modern literature.* She referred elsewhere in her letters to the *mediocre moderns.*

Thomas Hardy

Strong disagreement about Hardy's poetry. I had tried to read his *Collected Poems* from Blackwell's box but I found them overworked. I felt that, like John Bayley, she agreed with Hardy's idea of himself as really being a poet writing novels for money – as snobbish as Shakespeare thinking himself a lyric poet writing plays for money. I argued that Hardy's poetry doesn't 'sing', that it was a sort of 'joinery' using words, and the painful way it is constructed stops it singing. I divided writers into fast and slow and stuck up for my favourites – the fast natural writers like Shakespeare and Dickens and even P.G. Wodehouse! – and surely IM? – versus the slow writers whose work is a sort of joinery. She wasn't convinced.

IM as Poet

She distinguished poets from prose writers by calling poets *songsters*. This irritated me because she seemed to be saying that the difference lay in some twittering, musical quality. Regarding Hardy, she seemed to be saying that this *major poet* didn't stoop to the *light* music aspect of the *songsters*. She often said she wished she could write poetry, but worried that she wasn't *enough* of a songster, which was confusing.[28] Her published poems reveal that she was patently not a poet, precisely because her verse doesn't sing. I got the impression she thought prose-writers could work themselves up to poetry, like a kettle being brought to the boil.

It's pretty sweeping to say she wasn't a poet. It would certainly be too sweeping to say she didn't have an *ear* for poetry. She pounced on any line I misquoted – Saint Mary Woolnoth, for example, 'keeping' not 'telling' the hours in the Eliot poem.[29] That could just have been correcting a mistake rather than restoring a bit of botched music. But what convinces me she heard the music, at least in other people's poetry, is her last letter, where she remembers the Scottish folk-rhyme where rivers boast of their drowning powers … '*Said Tweed to Till, Why gar ye rin sae still*?' It showed an exquisite ear and total recall. On the other hand, could it just have been one of the jingles she and John knew by heart and chanted to each other? The most surprising example of her ear for words was when I misquoted the 1960 Paul Vance song as: 'She wore an itsy*witsy* teenie weenie yellow polka dot bikini':

IM: *No! it's 'ITSY BITSY'*, and, of course, she was right.

The Writing Contest

I had been reading about automatic writing produced by

[28] See *Poems by Iris Murdoch*, edited by Yozo Moroya and Paul Hullah (1997).

[29] T.S. Eliot, *The Waste Land*, 1, 'The Burial of the Dead,' line 67.

mediums at seances and asked her whether she thought anything good could be produced like this. Knowing her contempt for psychic research, I thought she would pour scorn on the idea, but she seemed game to have a go. In a following letter she said, *Yes, I have written things in such trances. I can versify endlessly when a bit drunk. We must have a poetry contest some time. What an odd thing the mind is!*

A few evenings later we sat on the sofa at Harcourt Terrace, got drunk, and had our contest. We each wrote a poem impromptu using free association; that is, we each produced about fourteen lines of gibberish, (why they both came out sonnet length I can't explain.) Hers was genuinely impromptu, mine was faked, because I had been expecting the contest and – frightened of drying up and sitting next to her with a blank piece of paper – I had been practising. Not as cunningly as I had worked on my prepared answer to the God question if it came up, but enough to get by and feel a bit guilty. How many young men of 24 have played writing games with a famous novelist, even if they cheated? It confirms John Bayley's description of how joyfully she could fling herself into things like this – she was delighted by the results. I have kept both bits of paper (see pages 124-127).

Letting Go

DM: 'Why don't you pull all the stops out?'
IM: *As a writer you mean?*
DM: 'Yes – Dickens, Yeats, Joyce, even Kipling pull all the stops out, but you seem to hold back; there's always a sort of gentility. Dickens, the 'criminal,' can tear the reader's heart out. I cry when I read him, and when I read Joyce, but I have never cried reading you.'
IM: *Yes – I know.*

I think this conversation coincided with one of her moments of despair at not being able to crank herself up to the next level – at not being able to 'draw blood' as a writer – and she had gone to Canetti for advice. By a fluke he said the same thing – that she should let rip more – and she gave the same reply – that she was afraid of hurting or offending people. She also said she didn't know how to, but I got the impression that, deep down, she still felt it would be over-the-top, too 'me'-centred, and that she should hold back. As you know, she disapproved of the subconscious mind as a source of art if it was allowed to take over – she thought it was full of bad stuff – but I knew at the same time she was cutting herself off from a rich and terrible source that had empowered male writers. It was how they pulled the stops out.

Titles

I was telling her how my daughter, aged thirteen, had found herself surrounded by old women when she went for a ballet test at White Lodge in Richmond Park, and how they were pulling her about to see if she was supple enough. I said, 'It was like seeing Angharad among the witches'. IM (immediate interest in the image and the ring of the words) – *'That would make a good title.'*

Shakespeare

DM: 'I've been trying to work out who "Mr W.H." was – you know – with the eye of the uneducated'.
IM: *You might just get somewhere like that.*
DM: 'What do *you* think? Was it the Earl of Southampton?'
IM: *Well, you've got to realise his predicament – placating all these grandees.*

To get her talking, I tried the 'Is he a good writer?' ploy and she launched into an exposition of why Shakespeare was a good writer. It was inspired, as if she was giving a lecture, but better because impromptu. Not unlike the scene in your *Life* where Donald Mackinnon holds forth in a pub, a hush falls and the customers cheer. The pub in this case also fell silent. She adulated Shakespeare more then she adulated Titian and probably more than she adulated dogs. I think there is a long eulogy of Shakespeare in one of her novels (you'll know where).[30] Like that, it was a *tour de force* and it left me breathless. It's preserved in written form in the novel but that is only a paraphrase of what I heard.

DM: 'But what about the bad writing in Shakespeare?'
IM: *You've got to realise he was like a TV scriptwriter with Burbage standing over him saying, "Come on Bill".*

I pestered her again about the sonnets and I got the impression that she thought they were probably duty-love-poems to his patron; that is, literary exercises.

Like many of the self-taught I was always coming up with strange facts:

DM: 'I've just read that, at the end of one of his plays, Shakespeare had to line up with the actors and do a jig!'
IM: *Yes, but only if he was acting in it. And anyway it would have been a* -------.

She used a fancy French or Italian term like *allemande* or *balletto*, which presented a more acceptable picture of Shakespeare not having to do much more than incline his leg gracefully a few times in front of the audience. I remember being impressed, but faintly irritated, by her pedantry in the same way that later, 'Tan Tan' rather than 'Tin Tin' jarred. I could add that her frenchifying was sometimes a source of panic when she ended her letters with *au revoir* because I couldn't remember whether it meant 'till next time' or 'goodbye' (*adieu*).

30 Possibly the discussions of *Hamlet* in *The Black Prince* (1973).

She Irritates

I sometimes found her ponderousness trying – but particularly the ponderousness of her chums. I was at Harcourt Terrace once when the phone rang and the most ridiculous conversation ensued. The friend wouldn't say who it was (expecting to be recognised by voice alone) and IM wouldn't admit she didn't know who it was. They fenced with one another for several minutes, with the friend becoming more and more insistent on being recognised and IM more and more flustered at not recognising her…

IM: *Oh – gosh – yes – of course I do – err – yerrs – errr…* (not a clue).

She never got round to saying, *Who is it?* and the friend never got round to saying who it was. The phone was put down after an act of complete non-communication, but by the rules of the game they had to pretend communication had taken place. On Iris's part, it was an example of her courtesy, but I was becoming so impatient with the whole patrician thing and its overly-polite exchanges that I was inclined to see it less as courtesy and more as farting about. From the degree of farting I deduced this was an Oxford chum.

On another occasion I arrived at Harcourt Terrace and was introduced to a grandee chum – a tweedy, rollicking woman paying a flying visit – who may have been the original of the 'Margot' referred to in John Bayley's trilogy.[31] There was no faffing here; she was giving Iris a sort of report from the shires, telling her how they'd been out with the beagles on Sunday. I had already been saddened by the silliness she'd been dragged into by the Oxford chum. I definitely did not like the idea of her knowing beagle woman.

[31] John Bayley wrote three memoirs after his wife's death: *Iris: A Memoir of Iris Murdoch* (1998); *Iris and the Friends* (1999) and *Widower's House* (2001).

I Couldn't Call Her Iris

Oddly, when it came to this particular thing, I experienced the same inability to be straight that I'm castigating her chums for. Her letters to me begin, *Dear David, David you chump, David dear*, even *David darling*, but through some timidity on my part, I could never begin a letter 'Dear Iris' and never called her 'Iris' at meetings. On the one occasion I phoned her – the morning after the Six Day War – I couldn't say 'Iris' over the phone. I kick myself now for being so formal when I read that other people were greeting her, in jolly fashion, as 'Iris old girl ' and 'Ducky'.

It was the Wrong Name

Part of the problem was that (echoes of maladjustment) I was still blocking everybody out, including their names. But it was also that I never felt her name fitted. To me she was a 'Jean', with its tawny, tough, Scots connotations. 'Iris' was the name of a rainbow sylph full of shimmering blues. I felt it was less than straight of her not to write as plain Jean Murdoch.

Yeats

I referred to Yeats a lot, a poet whose lines rang in my head. But there was no eulogy, like the outburst about Shakespeare. Was there even a trace of disparagement? In a letter about my attempts to get to university to do English, she warned me that English might consist of studying Dryden rather than *'brooding about Yeats, whom you already understand'*.[32]

[32] The novels show familiarity with Yeats: Emma Sands quotes the line from 'The Spur' about 'lust and rage' in *An Unofficial Rose* (1962); a line from '*A Prayer for my Daughter*' about 'a house/ Where all's accustomed, ceremonious' is echoed in *The Sacred and Profane Love Machine* (1974).

Violence

She hadn't quite talked me out of violence and thinking to stump her I quoted Yeats: 'Even the wisest man grows tense/ With some sort of violence/ Before he can accomplish fate/ Know his work, or choose his mate.'

IM: *Yes, but he only says* *grows* *tense.*

IM: *Your revenge fantasies have nothing to do with 'virility' or 'manhood', but are connected with what's muddled or muddy in you. They will hinder your efforts to resemble Piero.*

Piero was, of course, Piero della Francesca, whose book had lain between us like a drawn sword. '*Being like Piero*' must have been part of some reform programme she had in mind for me, but it existed more in her mind than mine. I can't remember many efforts in that direction, or even that I'd agreed to make any. His calm, majestic example wasn't going to stop me punching people. In the end, realising that I was never going to resemble Piero, she settled for a mysterious compromise called 'orderly behaviour'. I wasn't sure what this was but I had no intention of going along with that either.

Revenge

Regarding revenge, I think she was shocked, not by revenge itself, but the fact of it involving physical violence. (Remember her horror at members of staff at the RCA hitting each other.) As an example of a more intellectual kind of revenge she cited a novelist she knew, whose revenge against a man who had gone off with his wife was to put him in a novel and minutely describe his teeth.

Man of Action versus the Effete

I saw myself as a man of action, compared with IM's circle, and her chums as precious. They would go in for academic bickering, but to hit each other went against some pacifist, conchie Oxford thing that I would have liked to rock to the core. They had already irritated me at Harcourt Terrace by their inability to say straight out on the phone who they were, and I imagined the same fencing and farting about being carried into every corner of their lives. I didn't include IM in this, only her chums. IM, I felt, could be quite physical if pushed.

IM: *Hitting people is something one must be so damn careful about. Maybe I'll hit you one day.*

To pique her interest I reported occasional bits of violence on my part – girl-slapping and tussles with men that usually involved hair-pulling and thumb-twisting. The most violent thing I reported – '*What you wrote made my hair stand on end*' – consisted of going to another college with a stick on a revenge mission. My victim was a harmless boy who had tumbled inconclusively into bed with one of my lovers where effectively nothing happened. I over-reacted and went on a vendetta. It was one of those things that nothing could *stop* you doing, blindly even triumphally, when you are young, and which years later blinds you a second time – by its 'littleness' and the way it wrecked things.

Thankfully, I never hit him, but instead used the stick on some railings in the forecourt which went down like nine-pins. I remember the principal sticking his head out of the building, then pulling it back in like the captain of a beseiged castle. How I wasn't arrested I don't know. I realise now it wasn't just an attack on a college student, but on an elitist higher education system itself. In fact, on the art world – which I had fraudulently managed to get into, but in which I couldn't cope. Hence my irritation at IM's exhortations to

Paint! and at her obtuseness at not seeing that what I wanted to do was *write*.

Some scrap of self-preservation stopped me telling Iris the full story or the refined cruelty of the sequel involving the pair (nor can it be told here), but even the shortened account had more than the desired effect – and her reaction was on the same scale as her reaction to the Keith affair. She gave me a terrible ticking off, demanding that I apologise to the people concerned, but of course I didn't.

These notes aren't a confessional. They are evidence of how damaged I was at 24 and the scale of what she was taking on, trying to help me. Not, as it turned out, without dangers to her reputation.

Damned Queneau

IM: *Damn Queneau. He let the boot of a car crash down on my head at Orly Airport – I still have the scar.*

She showed me a small scar on her forehead near the hairline, and was still quite angry about it all these years later. It was so small I could hardly see it.

Dylan Thomas

I asked her about Dylan Thomas. She had met him at parties, and she surprised me by saying plummily, Did you know Dylan? How could I possibly have known Dylan Thomas? When he died I was a thirteen-year-old boy in Birmingham. I supposed at the time that this was another example of her wandering gravitas, but was also a bit put out that she was so unfocused on who she was with that she could make the mistake. Looking back, I have realised she was just saying the first thing that came into her head, through shyness. She was often shy at meetings, sometimes stammeringly so. I think I muttered something about, no, not actually meeting him, but I'd heard that his wife,

Caitlin, threw herself out of a window in Manresa Road (true). We were both so flustered that she never got round to telling me about him, but I could tell she liked his work. I didn't – I thought it was a sort of sonorous fake poetry. This was another example, I thought, of her odd taste in poetry – a case of a good writer, but one who was a non-poet, being fooled by what looked like poetry on the surface.

Sartre

Your *Life* records IM meeting Sartre twice in Paris in 1945, first at a lecture and then the next day at a café *soirée.* What she told me was that she tried to meet him privately by going round to his flat in Paris, but Simone de Beauvoir wouldn't let her in. I got the impression that de Beauvoir wasn't just protecting the master – she was sexually jealous.

The Wittgenstein Puzzle

We know she met Wittgenstein in 1954 at Cambridge. Why are accounts so muted? They record a stilted exchange about apples that reads like a pupil-meets-master cliché: 'You have come for apples from my tree'. But far from the naked confrontation of personalities you mention in your *Life,* my impression is just of two people feeling uncomfortable at what should have been the big moment. His bare room and his domineering personality should have added up to a god-zone she trembled to enter, but my impression from talking to her was that she didn't tremble – she just felt uncomfortable.

I tried to bring her out about Wittgenstein. I thought she would have a lot to say; I might even get a *tour-de-force* like the one on Shakespeare. But she mumbled and wouldn't be drawn. Could it be that she instinctively disliked him as she had Koestler? Or that she did not understand him? Or understood him and disagreed violently, but kept quiet because he was a world figure? Or was it just that Elizabeth Anscombe had got there first? Or did he just belong to the rival firm?

She knew the legends. She used his voice in three novels.[33] She gave his characteristics to her mad philosophers. She may have based her enchanter figures on the way he took people over. But there's something missing about the moment they met. Where is the shiver? Where is the coming into the presence I experienced when we met Father Irvine? Did she downplay the meeting for some reason? Not own up to awe? Not allow him to be God because he had disparaged those men closest to her heart – the refugee Jewish academics?[34]

Her silence on the subject of Wittgenstein was a bristling silence like the last sentence of his 'Tractatus': 'What we cannot speak of we must pass over in silence.'

Heidegger

Among the questions I want to ask her, as if she's still there, is obviously, 'Why not Wittgenstein?' But a much deeper question is 'Why Heidegger?' 'Why did it all come back to Heidegger?' 'What had he got?' 'Why did he beat you?' (Seven years' work – scrapped book.)[35]

Cocteau and Camelot

My first teaching job, which only lasted a year, was at a small country art school in Gloucester; it's now closed:

[33] Wittgenstein is present in *The Black Prince, A Word Child* and *The Good Apprentice*. *Nuns and Soldiers* opens with his name and he is also in the background of both *Under the Net* and *The Message to the Planet*.

[34] Conradi states that IM 'later spoke of [Wittgenstein] as evil; he abandoned old friends, harshly criticised Jewish refugee philosophers'. (*IMAL*, p.263.) He didn't specifically attack the Jews she revered: Fraenkel, Steiner or Canetti, and they weren't 'philosophers', but I feel they were included in the sweep of his contempt. (DM)

[35] Murdoch's Heidegger manuscript, acquired by the Centre for Iris

DM: 'I'm going to show Cocteau's *Orphée* to my students at Gloucester.'
IM: *It's one of the three or four films in the world that I love.*
DM: 'Do you still go to the pictures?'
IM: *It's years since I stopped going to films.*

But, in 1976, she told me she and a friend were going to see a big film – *Camelot*, with Richard Harris as King Arthur and Vanessa Redgrave as Guinevere, based on the New York musical. I got the impression that the friend was a woman, and their trip to the cinema to see this rubbish was going to be a serious expedition.

IM's going to see *Camelot* was a surprise. You must remember that at the time – before the balance of power shifted and I began to see her as vulnerable – I was the *ingénu* and she was the sophisticate. *Camelot* was the first of a series of little incidents that showed me how innocent she was. She wasn't going to see it as light relief; I think she set out to see a singing Richard Harris, believing it would be as deep an experience as the *Morte d'Arthur* or the *Mabinogion*.

Insults

DM: 'I can't let myself be insulted.'
IM: *Nor can I.*

This and several other comments go against the idea of 'Saint Iris' as remembered in John Bayley's book, and by others. I was always aware of a fierce side to IM, revealing Irish pride and temper. We get a flash of it on page 481 of your *Life* – *'My absolute Luciferian pride'* – when Brigid Brophy accused her of dishonesty. And I had got a flash of it when I made her look a fool over the testimonial:

Murdoch Studies, is in the Conradi Archive, in the Murdoch Archives at Kingston University. The first chapter is to be published in *Iris Murdoch: Philosopher*, edited by Justin Broackes (OUP, forthcoming).

IM: *I'm not in a mood to be amused by your blunders. I dislike being made to look stupid.*

When I told her about trying to teach louts who misbehaved, she said:

IM: *It's like your telling me that you had undergone some awful insult. I would myself feel so insulted by this behaviour I would become very angry.*

A bit of an overreaction – they were only country boys mucking about. She advised me to *dominate them, tiger-trainer wise.*

Anything and Everything (2)

Reynolds Stone? -- IM: *I'm full of mortality tonight – a friend of mine has just died.*

This was circa 1979 – was she referring to the death of RS? [36]

The impossibility of paying. I've described how she threatened to scream when I made a feeble effort to pay in the Bizarro Restaurant. I remember us comparing notes and you saying she would never let you pay either.

Puritan – IM: *I'm a puritan.*
DM: 'I'm a puritan who always says, "yes".'

One of the things I am trying to work out is how the promiscuity referred to in the biographies co-existed with the 'idealistic puritanism' inherited from her Scots forebears.

[36] Alan Reynolds Stone (1900-1979), engraver, designer and typographer, who was a lifelong friend of John Bayley and Iris Murdoch.

Nazi – DM: 'I'm a Nazi.'
IM: (Giving it serious consideration as a proposition) *Are you really?*

We both hated America -- I was inveighing against it for some reason…

IM: *America, oh, it's so – sick.*

Myth – IM: *Myth is the great temptation.*

Perversion and Women

As a preamble to confessing what I thought was perverted behaviour on my part, as a member of the 'dirtier' sex…

DM: 'Women can't be perverts, can they?'
IM: *Of course they can!*

IM: *Women are people.*
DM: 'I wasn't convinced'.

Trouble

IM: *You like trouble.*

Yes, I did. But I think she did too. She liked intrigue, as both observer and participant. And I might even dare to suggest it in relation to the Keith incident. She was terribly upset by it. She tried to help. She was dangerously involved in a situation that could have led to him failing and her resigning – on a different scale from the triangle she had got herself involved in with me and my girlfriends. I know I said earlier that it was so awful it couldn't have contained a vicarious thrill for anybody but, if I go over it again, I wonder whether, as the trouble was scaled up, so perhaps was her unconscious excitement.

Bad Manners

IM: *I'm mildly annoyed with you. You should have stood up for David Hicks in the Duke of York.*

Feeling rather grand as IM's protégé, I had remained seated. There then followed a nonsensical argument between IM, David Hicks and me on the subject of 'perks'. They maintained that if life gave one any breaks it was right to make the most of them; I maintained that it was Spartan and correct not to. It was a daft conversation and I don't know how it started, but I was a bit surprised that IM the puritan should side with David Hicks on this. Correction – the first part of my behaviour was OK – I had stood up. The second part was not: I had seated myself before David Hicks sat down.

Aesthetic Experience

IM: *One can only have an aesthetic experience in one theatre of sense at a time.*

As I have said, my thesis had been on how Welsh revivalists worked up crowds, and it went on to study the pathological effect of oratory on crowds in general, including the way Hitler combined oratory with pageants, lights and singing. From that we had got on to multi-media, where a work of art tries to appeal to all the senses at once, as in opera. But for her, opera couldn't work – it fired on too many cylinders. I tried to stump her with Wagner and his 'Gestamtkunstwerk' (total work of art). Surely Wagner works? No – he didn't – he was clearly not her cup of tea.

Religion

IM: *What do you think about religion?* (Not the usual, '*Do you believe in God?'* you mention her confronting strangers with.)

DM: 'I don't believe in God but I believe in Christ as a bodhisattva.'

I was pleased with this reply; it was probably cooked up beforehand in case the '*What do you believe?*' question came up. It was one of the few times I faked anything. She had mentioned an interest in Buddhism as far back as the early '60s. Buddhist in religion; Liberal Democrat in politics. From reading your book I see the Christ is Buddha idea was going the rounds.

Marriage

IM: *I hesitated and hesitated, although I had loads of proposals.*

She then listed some, including the mysterious 'Tom Rothschild' I mentioned. This was when she referred to having been pursued until she wore her admirer out, and to *having been told for so long in the most extravagant terms that I am beautiful.* For a woman who was so self-abnegating she had a definite sense of her sexual worth, and one of my problems is to understand her intellectual and sexual submission to her Jewish 'masters', whom books portray as gargoyles. ('She had the ugliest boyfriends of any of us'.)[37] Her confident sexuality seemed to go with her Irish pride, which made these prostrations all the odder.

Mrs Bayley, Who?

When she first wrote out a cheque for me, the painterly blue signature said, not 'Iris Murdoch' but, 'Mrs Jean

[37] This remark was made by a female contemporary of Murdoch during *Iris Murdoch, Strange Love* (Omnibus, BBC 1, 2002).

Bayley'. Who on earth was she? Why did Iris Murdoch sign cheques as a woman married to a man called Bayley? Why didn't she have a bank account in her own name? Her deference to John Bayley was even harder to accept when I learnt more about him, because his puckishness seemed not to merit it. How, for example, could she have so meekly let Bayley insist she leave Oxford to break up the lesbian affair,[38] or so meekly take on his literary tastes? I was not happy about her being part of a Bayley double-act, and the cheque confirmed it in writing.

JB / JB reading

IM: *I have, by the way, mentioned your existence in general terms to John Bayley, but he doesn't want to know details.*

This was slightly odd. Sitting on her sofa at Harcourt Terrace she had (as mentioned) said, *You must let me make the rules, For example, you can't go to bed with me.* That was clear-cut and I was happy for it to be platonic. But if it was to be so innocent, why did Bayley not wish to know details? Unconsciously, coquettishly, did she want him to think there was more to it than there was?

IM: *John reads books by breaking them apart.* (That is, so keenly that the act of reading destroyed the book.) I was impressed by this image of how Oxford people read, and she said it admiringly.

Henry James

John Bayley raved about *The Golden Bowl* and she referred to it as *this great shimmering thing.*

I have a problem with *The Golden Bowl.* These notes are based on Iris as I knew her. I want to stick to *my* impres-

[38] See *IMAL*, pp. 456-459.

sions based on meeting and talking. I don't want to be forced to a re-think by the books that have come out since her death. They can't change my picture much, but they must change it a bit and, if I had known more about the Oxford end, these notes might have been less reverential. The London Iris of the '60s and '70s was a brave figure who rushed about helping people – listening to them, paying for them, educating them, bucking them up, making them believe in themselves – a figure very much in charge. But the books are trying to persuade me that when she got on the train back to Oxford she turned into a different person – one who was much less in charge, and who – in A.N. Wilson's account of the Bayleys as Oxford's favourite eccentrics with their pet names and baby talk – seems to have joined JB in a sort of silliness *á deux*.[39]

My problem with *The Golden Bowl* is connected with the problem of John Bayley. Any men IM was fond of have problems with Bayley, because they are liable to be unconsciously jealous. It's almost a case of 'Why did he become the soul-mate and not *me*?' How could someone so deep submit to someone else's tastes so meekly, including his taste in literature? So the problem I have with *The Golden Bowl* is that John Bayley liked it and IM might – just might – have liked it so much because he did.

Angel Dream[40]

You quote a longer version in your *Life*. In the version she

[39] Was it confined to the Oxford end, or did something akin to this baby talk with John find its way into her work? Am I hearing it, for example, in the mawkishness of the diminutives in *A Word Child:* 'Tomkins' . . . 'Tomikins'. . .'Biscuit'. . 'Biconetta'. . . and – excruciatingly – in the leap frog scene in the snow in the same novel? Does this explain bits of writing, among wonderful writing, that have occasionally made me wince? (DM)

[40] Murdoch had 'dreams of holiness', or what Conradi describes as 'waking visions' all her life, which she sometimes gave to her characters. The dream, or vision, to which David Morgan refers here, occurred on 20th January 1947. Murdoch saw, in a garden, two allegorical birds

told me the angels didn't have gryphon-like birds' heads; she simply chased them and asked them the big question – *Is there a God*? Incidentally, a possible source for the figures in your version could be the *Orphée* films of Cocteau we know she liked. Do you recall the image in one of them of a sort of white feathered sphinx moving along on the other side of a hedge?

Severed Heads

I knew she was shy and could be frosty but I didn't know about the famous reserve, so didn't realise how privileged I was when she let her hair down with me. A game we played was to let our minds run freely over subjects that ranged from the crashing sound the Severn Bore made as it approached Gloucester (which she had witnessed as a child on a school-trip from Bristol) to headhunting.

It almost turned into a game like the poetry contest. Then we improvised words wildly; here we came up with the craziest subjects we could think of and gabbled all we knew about them to each other. Once she got going, she turned out to be as capable of the uncensored as anything I came up with. Sometimes the ideas would be continued in a letter. As an example, we had been to an exhibition of African masks, which got me onto the subject of the life-mask I wanted to make of her. From that we got onto head-hunting and from that to severed heads and the rites practised with them. From there we went on to a particular tribe that cuts heads off and makes them perform fellatio. She continued in a letter as follows:

of prey who transmuted into winged angels with golden hair. They come down from their pillars and Murdoch follows them and asks, 'Is there a God?' to which they reply, 'Yes'. (For a fuller description of this dream, see *IMAL*, pp. 554-55.) Murdoch gives a version of it to the former nun, Anne Cavidge, in *Nuns and Soldiers* (1980), and to the spiritual seeker, Bellamy James, in *The Green Knight* (1993).

IM: *Your fellatio idea is very powerful. No – it was never in my mind; I was thinking more of eye-to-eye contact with them and the Medusa/genitals link. You have a more blasphemous and obscene mind than I have.*

We ended by planning a severed-head tour of London but it never happened.

Sexual Taboos and Tableaux

In my 'rape' report to Iris I had been a victim, or part-victim, but when I reported sex in which I took the dominant role, her response was interesting. If I reported attempts to dominate or to limit somebody else's freedom *outside* sex, she came down on me like a ton of bricks. But domination *inside* sex seemed to be OK, so was debasement and submission. Doing and being done were necessary positions that the tableau demanded; it included everybody in every position and this was a joyful thing. But – perhaps because it broke rules of decorum – it was something to be secretive about.

When we talked about sex she became conspiratorial, always urging a full confession, as in the rape report, to the point where even I held back the goriest details. At first this seemed prurient, until one realised she saw sex differently. I saw it either in terms of 'scoring' (quick encounters), or as something more drawn-out that usually went wrong as soon as I got close enough to a woman to start meddling with her hormones. Women made me uneasy, as people who were emotionally and physically out of control – and out TO control. They had the frightening capacity to flip at any moment and I remembered with horror the way my own mother, when crossed, would explode psychologically when I was a boy. They also had the ability to make one lose control of oneself by falling in love with them, as I had done. To get some control back, my attitude to them became sadistic. I saw sex as a way to dominate them – as, in fact, the only chance one got to do so (an attitude I only shook off ten years later with the birth of my daughter, the beloved dedicatee of these notes).

I was honest with Iris about these feelings. They broke all her rules and should have outraged her, but apart from the mild *Women are people*, or *Your anti-women diatribe was too rubbishy for comment*, she let me get away with it and often wanted to hear more.

I was so naïve that initially I didn't think of her as a sexual being at all and was puzzled at her interest in my sex life. I put it down, as I mention somewhere else, to her natural curiosity as a novelist and thought she might be collecting material or something like that. The kissing, early in the relationship, had not been sexual kissing on my part – not even 'aunty' kissing. I can say with a straight face that it had been equivalent to placing my lips against a sibyl's – something as cold and thrilling and as remote.

Books published since then have shown me she was full-bloodedly into sex and it came as a shock. She liked sex and she thrilled at hearing about sex and, as I have tried clumsily to explain, she suspended her rules about civility, kindness and respect during the act itself in case this limited the tantric force of the encounter – an entanglement that became more and more exciting the more complicated it became. She liked her friends' lives to be as convoluted as possible, even though she took on the contradictory role of helping sort them out. She mixed and match-made and intrigued to get people as mixed up together as she could. (Read A.N. Wilson's hilarious account of her and John Bayley masterminding his affair with Katherine Duncan Jones and spying on its progress from their Volkswagon.) When people let her down and followed their natural instinct to be monogamous and faithful and dull, she whirled them together artificially in her books to create what one critic described as 'sexual square dances'. Iris Murdoch liked stirring it. But it was a creative sort of stirring, reminding one of that Indian god who churned a world out of nothing.[41]

A Tableau

Increasingly, my own affairs had nothing joyful or tantric to report. They consisted of the dogged pursuit of Magda and the consequent two-timing of Paulette – two women made miserable. They might still make a pretty pattern in Iris's eyes – with all that magical nonsense she attributed to them – but they had, for me, turned into an unhappy stalemate. There was also a string of meaningless one-night stands I never told her about, because they might have spoiled the shape of the suffering threesome that had got her so interested in the first place. Oddly, for someone who had been such a sexual show-off, another reason I didn't tell her about them was because I thought she might think of me as a rake, not pursuing my suffering seriously enough.

I thought it would only be a matter of time before she moved on and interested herself in a new set of people who were making a more exciting shape with their lives. I imagined them already there, like gymnasts frozen in some complicated position calculated to excite, waiting their turn in the future.

Then, in an unplanned fashion, something occurred that *would* interest her. Things fell into place in a fresh way, involving not two women and myself, but two men and Paulette. It happened a few weeks after the trouble with Keith. I was pretty chastened where he was concerned and, as I have described, we were anyway on better terms. The same sick urge to dominate a situation – which dated from having been so helpless in the hospital – was still

[41] Hindu story of creation, 'Churning the Ocean of Milk' in which gods and demons, directed by Vishnu and Shiva, join forces and stir the world back into being after one of its periods of nothingness. (DM)

there though, and I indulged in a bout of one-upmanship with another student from the RCA. Paulette and I and the student were in the Ladbroke Grove flat one afternoon when out of the blue I 'gave' Paulette to him. I did it partly out of an impish urge to see what would happen, partly out of the old pathological urge to pull the strings. It's a bit hazy, but I do remember that part of the excitement was actually saying, 'Do you want to f--- Paulette?' and watching their reaction. I planned not to join but watch.

Paulette was nonplussed at first, but was now so resigned to her role as victim that she went along with it and didn't protest. The student was also nonplussed, not sure whether he was getting one up on me by 'taking' my woman or losing face because he was being given her on a plate. There was a mattress on the floor and they grappled on it a bit unenthusiastically, but then I lost my nerve and called a halt, using the excuse that he had no contraceptives, at which they sprang apart. All this was duly described to Iris and, so far from telling me off for playing with people, she responded immediately and visually to the shapes the three of us made and what was going on in our heads. She even pursued this in a letter:

I would offer a different interpretation of their behaviour. I think they were somewhat frightened of you, or by you. If I had been there I would have been very excited and questioned you closely about what you saw and what on earth you intended.

Talking with the Dead

I raised the subject of séances:

DM: 'Do you believe in communication with the dead?'
IM: (scornfully) *No sensible message has ever come through, only the equivalent of dead birds in the bottom of a cupboard.*

This appears almost word for word in *The Nice and The*

Good.[42] She dismissed psychic research only a shade more contemptuously than she mistrusted the subconscious.

Bestiality

During the time I taught the country boys, as a lark I gave her lurid descriptions of people having sex with animals to see how she would react. It may have been because I was still trying to shock her, or because I knew she liked the bizarre. Or, I confess, it could just have been taking the mickey. Her ponderousness did sometimes tempt one to do this. To my surprise she took me seriously and weighed the moral pros and cons:

IM: *I think I would have to condemn it because we cannot be certain the animals consent, although of course in the case of a much loved dog the case may well be different.*

Jewish Sexuality

IM: *Do you find the Jews sexual too?* (Perhaps it was 'Jews' rather then 'the' Jews)
DM: 'Yes.'

I had always felt this and, for me, Honor Klein was her strongest character. On a lighter note, I had recently been almost debagged at the RCA by two Jewish sisters, and found myself incapable of meeting their demands in bed.

DM: 'Do you think it's because they have been a threatened race obeying a biological imperative to breed harder? I've read that bird species threatened with extinction try to outbreed death by frantic copulation.'
IM: *Errrr ummmmm.*

[42] In *The Nice and the Good* (1968) a cage of dead birds is found in a cellar in Whitehall, where they had been used for the black magic rituals of the Satanist, Radeechy.

Philo-Semitism with Reservations

On the morning Israel won the Six Day War in 1967, by destroying the Egyptian air-force on the ground, I saw it, romantically, as a David and Goliath struggle:

DM: 'Isn't it wonderful about the Jews?'
IM: (Far from chuffed – in fact damned critical) *Errr -yes – but what about the Arabs on the West Bank?*

Vote X

I knew her long enough for her politics to have swung different ways. As a hippy fellow-traveller, I was apolitical, seeing it all as a double XX, and I was too wrapped up in myself to be particularly interested in how she voted. Her letters to me seem to record her being Labour, Lib Dem and Tory in that order. A letter of the early '60s says, *Thank God for the Labour Party being in, or at least it looks as if they're in*. In the early 1980s another letter told me she was *probably* going to vote Liberal Democrat, which struck me as wishy-washy. By the late 1980s Lib. Dems were off the horizon and her rage against Labour over comprehensives, that had been bubbling since the 1960s, boiled over and we hear her urging – even *commanding* ANW to vote Tory. But just as I seem to be one of the few people she never faced head-on with her '*Do you believe in God*' question – so she never asked me how I was going to vote and certainly never told me how to. Meetings and letters dealt almost exclusively with the acutely personal and suffering particular, rather than these generalities. Or perhaps she thought I wasn't up to it.

IM Outed

It's important to repeat how separate she kept the London

and Oxford ends, and how as a naturally secretive person, she arranged her life so that she could shuttle between them and emerge as a different person at each end.[43]

At one end were her gang of 'artists, actors, art-students and London queens',[44] and all of whom could be loosely described as 'left'. At the other end were a gang of erstwhile lefty dons and grandees, her chums of the late 1930s, who seem to have gone through an over-correction (IM: *children that we were)* and metamorphosed into Tories in the late 1980s and '90s. If one marvels at the scope of her promiscuity – her capacity to be in love with several people at once – one must marvel at her ability to get on so well with the people at both ends, and switch so easily between their zeitgeists. I described in the earlier note how I felt she was 'strong' at the London end but meek at the other. ANW also picks up on the two Irises at different ends, but instead of my division into strong and meek, he sees a division into left and right. His London Iris hobnobs happily with her art students (me and the RCA crowd); his Oxford Iris, at least as described by him, seems to have been mysteriously, upsettingly comfortable in a circle of friends that contained people who 'thought Mrs Thatcher hadn't gone far enough'. And far from the meek figure deferring to JB, that I have pictured, she seems to have been blusteringly sociable in this group, even laying down the law, albeit a bit drunkenly, when it comes to voting. The most upsetting thing is what he calls the 'outing' of the Bayleys in old age as reactionaries which he describes with relish.[45] Not, I think, ANW but perhaps the reviewer of one of his books,

[43] One is reminded of Dickens's' secret life, shuttling by train between London and Slough, as Charles Dickens at one end and Charles Tringham at the other. (DM)

[44] ANW quoting his friend Pickles (*Iris Murdoch as I Knew Her* p. 215), among whom Pickles thought she was happiest. (DM)

[45] The article referred to was published in *Against the Grain*, Verso, 1986. See *Iris Murdoch: As I Knew Her* for A. N. Wilson's reference to it: 'I well recall the sense of shock caused in Oxford by Terry Eagleton's muted attack...etc'.

even refers to IM as a 'whooping Tory'. Oxford was necessarily remote and kept remote from me but this seems to be another Iris I have to come to terms with. But I want to put on record, as somebody who knew her and listened to her for thirty years, that she stuttered and stammered and ummm'd and errr'd and occasionally gosh'd and golly'd, but she never whooped in her life.

Subventions

DM: 'I'm in a mess financially: I owe three months rent.'
IM: *I'm a bit strapped for cash at the moment, dear boy – I'm paying school fees for my Irish cousins' children.*[46]

I remember her telling me they had red hair. I didn't know whether to imagine a gang of tinker children or red-haired young squireens. The low point – comedic and shameful – in the history of these subventions was reached when she wrote to me that she didn't keep cash in the house and had run around Steeple Aston for money, but the shops were shut.

Money/Sex

IM: *Money is sexual.*

I remember the sexual thrill of her slipping that £5 note into my pocket the first time I went to Harcourt Terrace. But I must stress that, apart from the playfulness at the first meeting, what you call 'frequent subventions' were not lavished on me. At the start of the relationship they were strictly applied for, based on need, and strictly issued; sometimes – as above – refused. I have to admit though that, as I grew bolder, what I portrayed as need began to verge on scrounging. I remember asking her for money for a

[46] Cf *IMAL*, where Conradi states that Murdoch's Bell first cousins believed their contact with Murdoch was minimal.

watch, prefaced by:
DM: 'I – um – need a watch so I'm not late for teaching. I'm thinking of getting a second-hand one.'
IM: (Falling for it.) *Err – don't do that Dear Boy – buy a new one – I'll give you the dough.*

Then she confounded me with her complete naïveté about cost by suggesting a sum that wouldn't have bought even a second-hand one. As another example, in 1965, I felt strongly that getting to see the eruption of the new volcano Surtsey, off the coast of Iceland, was an important part of my spiritual development, so tried to 'borrow' the fare. She refers erroneously in her diaries to me wanting to see Etna erupt. This time she wasn't having it.

When more serious, non-David needs arose later on, such as my daughter's schooling, I had grown out of the harum-scarum borrower of the early days, but I was forced, reluctantly, to borrow bigger amounts. She was consistently, wonderfully generous and fully up-to-date with the cost of things. She even paid two hundred pounds for her to be coached for the entrance exam to St Paul's Girls' School to save her from a comprehensive.

Giving and Taking

Re-reading these notes I find that even now, more than 40 years later, I am dramatizing myself as a rogue as I did with IM. I exaggerate the extent to which I was the taker and she the giver. I cadged shamelessly because I was hard up, but it wasn't all one way. I gave her a series of small gifts and I was always on the lookout for things that would interest her. The list of gifts included: IM to DM – money (lots of small amounts), the box of books from Blackwells, and the pair of gold-plated, lapis-lazuli cuff-links from Harrods. DM to IM – a netsuke philosopher, an inkwell shaped like a facetted glass pineapple and a radiometer. The radiometer was a spectacular object – a '60s optical toy in the form of a glass ball on a stand, containing a little rotating sail painted black and white which spun round in sunlight. She stood it on her desk and told me how it whizzed round while she wrote.

At one of the early meetings we went in for swapping. We were both wearing scarves – mine was yellow and black tartan; hers was a sort of chunky fawn tweed with a red stripe. '*Let's swap*!' she said. What she didn't know is that my scarf (a thin affair compared with hers) had already been through a swap. It had originally been round the neck of a mental patient in Rubery Hospital, and been the subject of some pretty hard bargaining. She went back to Oxford with it round her neck, and I had the reassuring sensation that somebody I had always felt I was on the point of losing was now 'tied' to me. One end of the scarf wound back to Ward 10; I held the other end and Iris was in the middle, capable of being wound in if she strayed too far. I waited expectantly for her to be wearing it at the next meeting but she wasn't.

If I wanted to be ingenious I could say that the scarf, and the way I imagined myself being able to pull on it, was a trial run for the way I dragged her into my relationships later on. She certainly accused me of doing this.

Suicide

The suicide of Carolyn de Ste Croix in 1964[47] coincided with my feeling pretty desperate myself. She quizzed me quite hard:

IM: *You wouldn't kill yourself would you?*
DM: 'No.'

She seemed satisfied by this.

[47] Carolyn de Ste Croix, daughter of the historian Geoffrey de St Croix, had been a student at St Anne's and a friend of Murdoch. She suffered from depression and when she killed herself Murdoch bitterly reproached herself for not having 'loved her better', she said in a letter to me. (DM)

Meet Carolyn

In your *Life* you mention Iris writing in her journal that after Carolyn's suicide she wished she had introduced her to Donald MacKinnon. She almost arranged a meeting between Carolyn and me, supposedly as two troubled people who might get on. But then she had second thoughts. I was always disappointed that she wouldn't introduce me to her younger women friends. Though unhappy, I was still enough of a Bluebeard to see her as a possible entrée to a supply of girls. I even went so far as to beg introductions to the daughters of friends. Like Canetti, she threw people together to see what would happen. Not, like him, sadistically, but ingenuously, like a child wanting to see them magically collide. In this case she was too loyal to their parents to take the risk. Carolyn must have been the exception because she was so far gone.

Incidentally, we had both put ladders up to girls' windows and climbed up (or had somebody climb up) in case the girl had killed herself, only to find the girl was out. I did this at the YWCA in the case of Magda.

My Painting / Her Painting

IM: *I wish some very traditional and stern master would stand over you and make you paint,* and then, more disturbingly, *If you can't do it for yourself – do it for ME.*

She told me she had been painting purple still-lifes. She knew her painting, like her poetry, was only amateur, but thought she was a better poet than a painter.

IM: *If I could paint properly I would for example, take a still life but show it in a strange light. Perhaps I have a frustrated painter in me that wants to come out in you.*

Poem in a Churchyard

For somebody who was supposed to be painting, I was writing more and more poetry and subjected her to quite a lot of it – lyric and concrete. I remember once, after a pub session in Soho, she took me to St Anne's churchyard so I could recite to her. We sat on a tombstone and I read her a long rambling poem in late Yeatsian ballad metre. I was expecting her to react the way Dame Edith Sitwell did to an early poem by Dylan Thomas (and as IM had done up to now – knock that painting thing on the head). But for once she was underwhelmed.

IM: *Yerrrs – I think, if I may say this, that it needs a bit more work, a little – errr – tuning here and there.*

For somebody who had been told that he was a considerable poet, this came as a bit of a shock. What was this thing about 'tuning'? I saw tuning as faking. It was a blow in another way. Apart from its scope for showing off, reciting poetry had also become a way I could capture her more completely as a woman. Although our relationship was platonic, I was as jealous of the people round her as if we had been lovers. I desperately wanted to be 'the One' in her eyes, and to be the one by overpowering her with words the way nobody else had ever done in her life. Poetry, as uttered by me, was going to cut through the intellectualising of the people (men) around her, straight to her heart. I would speak poetry to her till we swam in words and they almost sent her unconscious. This desire showed what should have been obvious to me much earlier – that there was a sexual sub-plot which had been going on for some time. We were now both aware of it, and its currency was words.

The only trouble was, this time it hadn't worked – the mesmerising spate needed 'tuning'. So I tried her with the other sort of poetry I was writing and read her three of my concrete sound poems[48] – 'Bebopalula', 'Breath song for a beloved', and 'Taketa Taketa', complete with bopping, breathing and clicking noises. This time she was completely baffled and didn't even soften the blow:

IM: *David – it seems to me that this is – errr – a preparation for something else, rather than the thing itself.*

Her new honesty was a turning point. She had always accused me of being slapdash, verging on bone-idle, when it came to things like getting a job, but had always praised me up when it came to art, even God help me, talking about us as if we were an artistic duo doing it side by side – and I believed her. But after my reading at St Anne's something had changed, and I didn't know why. All that had happened, of course, was that she had fallen sufficiently, fractionally out of love to come to her senses a little, and realise I was as slapdash about art as I was about life. Despite all my protestations, I was a lazy blighter when it came to both.

IM: *Such things must be worked on. I'm afraid you have a partic - ularly modern consciousness here and don't believe in discipline and order.*

Tomorrow

She had such a thing about my painting that I pretended to be doing it as well as banging out poems. In the end, she stopped urging me to paint, which was a relief because, as I have indicated, it was beginning to take the form of '*Paint, and I shall paint through you*!' which put me in a diffi-

48 An anti-lyrical approach where words are treated as things in themselves – gutteral sounds or concrete shapes on the page. The idea was to give language more punch so – like painting – it could directly affect the nervous system. I spent my final year at the RCA banging out this stuff on a typewriter. (DM)

cult position because basically I couldn't – I was a fraud as an art student. My ambition had been to do English at Oxford (all that reading). When this was scuppered, I found myself, two nervous breakdowns later, in Birmingham on the dole. I saw art school as a way out. Once in, the momentum carried me forward, and I couldn't stop because I would have lost my grant. It had even pushed me as far as applying to the Royal College of Art and I managed to wangle my way in. I wasn't a complete conman at the College, as it was called. I tried to paint in a ham-fisted way. But like the non-pianist who put his hands on a keyboard and knew that he would never play the piano, I knew I would never paint.

Despite now being a bit more honest about my poetry, particularly the concrete kind, in 1971 she put me in touch with some Oxford students who were starting a literary-cum-visual magazine called *Tomorrow*, backed by her and John Bayley. Six of my concrete poems were published and I designed the cover, which was based on deconstructing a Shakespearian sonnet. The students came to my flat in Ladbroke Grove to collect the poems. I showed them into my back room where I did my writing. The only odd feature here was a gas cooker jammed up against the bed which leaked gas very faintly – not enough to gas one, but enough to make going to bed each night a flirtation with death which never quite came off.

They sat on the bed, a bit puzzled by the smell of gas but quite charming. I'd never taken art students seriously but these were the real thing and I made the most of it. They knew nothing about concrete poetry and nothing about art, and the idea of mixing poetry and art in a magazine was clearly an adventure for them, with IM and John Bayley clucking encouragement in the background.

I tried to get them to stay as long as possible. They'd just come to pick up my poems but I saw it as a chance to talk, and I began to pour things out as I had done with IM. I think I saw them as IMs in miniature: sitting targets to bounce ideas off, ask questions of, air facts in front of. Some of these facts were the 'strange but true' kind autodidacts are so fond of; others I had got from reading about rubber-sheet geometry and mathematical paradoxes. I remember telling them about a family of two-dimensional creatures called the Mysterians, who could only slide over surfaces, and I demonstrated how they would slide round my room. I sensed them getting uncomfortable. Finally, one of them said, 'David you're a mine of the most perfectly strange information!' The *coup de grace*.

Re-reading *Tomorrow*, I see that undergraduate Andrew (A.N.) Wilson had also been approached, and that the poem at the back is by him.

Soap and Manuscript

With reference to her sending soap to a prisoner in Paris (in your *Life*), she told me not only that she had sent soap to somebody in prison but also that she gave him the manuscript of one of her early novels. She was pretty angry when she learnt he had sold this shortly afterwards. Who was this mysterious chap in prison?

IM and General Studies

General Studies at the RCA was just as much part of the old-boys' network as the painting tuition. In this case, Oxford chums (presumably chums of Christopher Cornford) were brought in to disseminate culture and they, in turn, brought in the Jewish teachers like Michael Kulmann and Frederic Samson whom I remember for their gloom and high intelligence. But Plato didn't travel well from Oxford to Cromwell Road. Lectures were ponderous and pedantic. Miss Anscombe, for example, had the gravitas of IM but not her aura. Michael Kulmann talked in a torrent that left one behind. The lectures and seminars were over the students' heads. Students laughing at poor old Samson pronouncing Kant 'Kunt' just about sums it up, and IM wrung her hands over being *just too academic for these kids.*

The bits of the syllabus that I remember were – Kierkegaard, Kant (philosophers): *Fear and Trembling* and *Critique of Pure Reason* and Stendhal and Dostoievski (novelists): *The Red and the Black* and *Brothers Karamazov.* You might ask why, if I was such an autodidact, didn't I take more in? Two reasons – first, it was boring, and I was enough of a 'panther' to want a more immediate *sensual* approach. Second, I was just too unhappy to concentrate, which is dealt with elsewhere.

IM as Teacher

How did IM fit in? Was she any good? Y-e-e-es, I would say she was. She struggled more than the others to get through. I remember only one sentence from her seminars:

IM: (cigarette in hand, illustrating a point) *If this cigarette was Sylvia…*

This got my attention. Sylvia and the cigarette coming together like this were the culmination of a struggle to make something clear which she'd had several shots at, missing each time, then nailing it with the metaphor. It was bumbling, as she had go after go and missed, but you could tell she was working out how much she'd missed by each time, homing in on the sentence that would get it across.

If she'd had a brighter bunch of students she would have been rated by Ofsted[49] as pretty effective, but only if you met her halfway. She could either grip you or lose you – grip you if you were prepared to circle round with her to get to the truth, lose you if you wanted straight answers.

[49] Ofsted is the Government body responsible for inspecting and regulating education and skills for learners of all ages.

Her tactic was to puzzle out a problem 'live' as if she didn't know the answer. This could involve mumbling discussions with herself which students could join in. Sometimes she would get the answer and sometimes she wouldn't. Sometimes the class would stumble on it themselves and realise with a shock that they had 'got' it. More often than not, they didn't – half of them were only there because General Studies was compulsory. I copied this trick (which I think she may have copied from Wittgenstein?) in my own teaching; it's always worked and never got me into a scrape, unlike some of her other methods.

One of the tips she gave me when I got my first job sounds very like bad teaching, and when I have brought it up in staffrooms and claimed it as my own, it has made eyes pop among the 'facilitators' of learning. In a letter she said, *Yes. I recommend a certain sadism, but ideally this sadism should be entirely veiled.*

Bad Teachers

We made the same mistakes as teachers. A girl at Oxford asked to be transferred because Miss Murdoch just talked about love; I was sacked for talking to the students about their sex-lives. Just as she copied MacKinnon lying on the floor to teach, I showed Cocteau's *Orphée* to my students at Gloucester by cleverly projecting it lying down, with students strewn round the floor. I also used her third degree approach, copied from Canetti (although I never asked them directly if they believed in God), and students in Hounslow soon told me in no uncertain terms this was 'taking a liberty'. Lastly, I came close to being sacked for bringing existentialism into History of Art. I showed a slide of Munch's *Scream* and got a girl to scream to it. It was so blood-curdling senior staff came running. In fact, most of IM's teaching tricks, as copied by me, got me into trouble, but I knew they were good teaching.

Lecture Nerves

DM: (quaking at giving his first lecture) 'Aren't you ever nervous in front of an audience?'
IM: *Phooey – I could address the Albert Hall.*

Hesitant, even stuttering sometimes in conversation, she seemed to have no nerves at all about public speaking. But on other occasions particularly referring to her RCA work she said, *I wish I wasn't so idiotically anxious about my lectures.*

IM as Male Impersonator

A.N. Wilson's description of her voice as the 'Voice of Wisdom itself' is perfect – this was exactly the sound. But what he misses is its faintly 'put on' quality. It was the way the voice of wisdom would sound if somebody had tried to imitate it. Was it partly imitated from the voices of MacKinnon and Fraenkel and Steiner? One hears a mock-pompous version of it in his account of facing Iris with a choice of two cakes … *I'll have to give this proposi - tion some thought...* But this was exactly the way she spoke. Even its pauses were like the pauses a male don might leave in order to puff his pipe while considering a problem. She had clearly adopted the way Queneau always paused carefully before replying.

She was wise – deeply wise – but it sounded as if at some point in the past, as a girl awed by male academia, she wanted to *sound* wise, so had unconsciously copied her professors. Many of her mannerisms seemed to be masquerading as something male. There was definitely a butch quality about Iris. I shan't forget how chuffed she was to be the first woman to give a lecture at Trinity, and, as I have described, it gave her sturdy satisfaction to give the Gifford lectures eight years after MacKinnon.

But she would have objected firmly to any accusation of being butch. I can't believe I ever dared refer to her in this way, but I must have done because she says in a letter, *Apropos my "gruff and neuter" persona* ... and completes this with a fuller version of the line quoted earlier: ... you must keep in mind that I have twenty-five years behind me of being told in the most extravagant terms that I am beautiful. I know this when you touch me ... etc.

This rejects the idea pretty firmly.

In odd contrast to the seriousness of the voice were its 'schoolgirl-isms'. She often used a sort of jolly-hockey-sticks language – *gosh, chump, dough, dolt, fathead, dammit, come off it, terrific ass, bounder, bad form, old thing*. Canetti sneered at this combination of 'schoolmistress and schoolgirl', and it could sound a bit St Trinian's; but it also evidenced a sort of simplicity which made her profoundly loveable.

LSD

I told IM *everything* – confessions, daily doings, reports from the front, and also snippets of anything that might interest her. I probably even hoped some might get into her books – and a couple did. I am responsible for the scintillating authenticity of Hilary Burde's LSD trip in *A Word Child*. She disapproved of drugs and never took them herself but I gave her detailed descriptions of my own trips. Her description of Mr Osmand's eyes, which had a thousand facets and each facet had a thousand facets, is based on my account of seeing a piano keyboard where each key had a thousand keys and each of those keys etc. One of my worst tickings-off was when I told her how I had given LSD to my cousin. Under its influence he had run off into Holland Park in the dark and

[50] *The Good Apprentice* (1985) opens with a student jumping to his death having been administered LSD without his knowledge.

realised WHO HE REALLY WAS, a revelation which had a disastrous effect on his job and marriage.[50] She thought I had done a fiendish thing – that to derange another human being's senses was literally the act of a fiend. She wouldn't listen when I told her he had been a willing party and referred to it gloomily over the years, asking how he was. What she never knew is that – attracted more by the mad enormity of it than any hope of making it happen – I wanted to break down her resistance and get Iris herself to take LSD, and to take it with her. I pictured us on a sofa at Harcourt Terrace, irradiated by rainbows, but as with a lot of my best ideas, sheer terror stopped me suggesting it.

Comforter

The morning after my father's funeral in Birmingham, I was back in my room in Ladbroke Grove. My door opened and IM came in carrying half a bottle of Teachers. How she had got in the house I don't know, and how did she know he'd died? She said nothing, just handed me the bottle. At a later meeting she told me how she had never got over her father's death and became visibly upset. Her appearing in my room like that was like one of the magical appearances in her novels, as if she'd come up through a trap door. Nothing was said, she just handed me the bottle and left.

My father had died, alone, in Birmingham, in slummy digs like mine. I had spoken often about him and she had sent him the odd inscribed copy of her novels. We had even compared the pedantic way our fathers spoke. When the telegram of his death came I had banged my head on the floor of my room in despair. I think I took for granted that she could appear out of nowhere like she did on that morning, but looking back on it – had she come all the way from Oxford? She'd been to an off-licence to buy the whisky – enough to deaden the pain. I went through the next couple of days in a groggy cloud thanks to the whisky. However many foibles, fallibilities, bits of patrician pride and occasional romancing these notes attribute to her, she was there for me when it mattered – Iris Murdoch and no other. Though she kept us all so separate, I would guess that she was there for each of us, when nobody else was, in the same way. I don't know why, but when I read in John Bayley's *Iris and the Friends* about her diving for his false teeth in Lake Como, I was reminded of her visit to my room thirty years earlier.

Touching, Close Up / Touching at a Distance

IM: *Wonderful stuff, skin.*

Her affection worked long distance. A couple of years after we first met I had an odd experience on Tamworth station. I had had a bad night chasing a woman who had shut her door in my face and had missed the last train back to Birmingham. I was trying to sleep on a bench, on the windy upper platform. Around Tamworth, in those days, was a pit landscape where my mother's ancestors had worked. Below me I could hear the rushing of the River Anker, which I had almost fallen into earlier in the evening. It began to rain and it was impossible to sleep. Suddenly, I experienced the sensation of a finger curling itself in my hair. Just that. It could have been the wind, but the touch and the affection were exactly how she'd touched me on the first night at Harcourt Terrace.

T. S. Eliot

You mention her wearing a man's peaked cap to meet Eliot in 1953 when she was canvassing for Janet Adam Smith as a possible new principal of St Anne's. I had read a bizarre account of somebody who had met Eliot and been surprised to see him wearing green make-up.

DM: 'When you met him, did he have green powder on his face?'[51]
IM: *No, he was perfectly normal.*

Apropos his poetry:

IM: *I think I am exactly the same age as Prufrock. Eliot helped a lot of people but I have always felt detached from him. I hope you can catch something of his floating spirit.'*

Oddly – as with Yeats – no eulogy. My impression was that both Yeats and Eliot left her a bit cold, which was odd because both were *dichter* figures who wrote magisterially, as if they were speaking from clouds, and seemed cut out to impress her. But there was something unsympathetic about each. Perhaps she was put off by Eliot's parsonifying and Yeats's hocus pocus. I *couldn't* understand it – what mattered to me was their music. I went round London t reading out their metre on the pavement. I had even come down from Birmingham, when I was eighteen, and stood outside Faber and Faber at two in the morning, looking up at a lighted window because Eliot might be behind it. But I felt she wasn't hearing it, which made me wonder again about her ear for poetry – for word music at the deepest level, where it becomes existence made song. This is quite separate from the baggage poets drag around with them, and which their art is supposedly based on, but which is really only there to get them going. Like the magical,

[51] This is not as far-fetched as it sounds. In *Painted Shadow* (2001), a life of Eliot's first wife Vivienne, Carole Seymour-Jones quotes accounts by Osbert Sitwell and Virginia Woolf of Eliot wearing green make-up and eye-shadow following the split-up with his wife and his return to a shadowy bachelor existence. The only explanation they could think of was that he was trying to look cadaverous to appeal for sympathy in his unhappiness. A more scurrilous later view is that they were seeing a secretly gay Eliot in 'drag'. (DM)

fascist, feudalist, Royalist, neo-Catholic, aristocratic mixed baggage of Yeats and Eliot. I felt that, not able to *just* listen, she may well have been put off by this.

She liked getting drunk. She got drunk on words with John Bayley. I couldn't understand why she couldn't get seriously drunk on these two.

Walking

(1) DM: 'Are you a good walker?'
IM: *Yerrs – not an heroic walker, but I walked all over London in the War.*

This must have been when she also told me she *drove ambulances in the War*, which you weren't convinced about.[52]

(2) She proposed we go together down the street somewhere (we normally went everywhere by taxi)[53] and I felt suddenly awkward and shy. Giving me my marching orders to stop mucking about and to walk beside her she said, '*What are you afraid of – do you think you'll fall apart?*'

(3)Walking next to her, obviously more confidently this time, I even found time to complain:
DM: 'The trouble with walking next to somebody is that you can't see them.'
IM, who obviously felt exactly the same frustration, agreed.

[52] The sister of Murdoch's flat-mate and friend Philippa Foot (née Bosanquet), Marion Daniel, drove a truck during the War bringing tea to Blitz victims (no driver's licence was required at that time). If Murdoch herself drove, it might have been with UNRRA in Austria, though no evidence has come to light.
[53] This contradicts A. N. Wilson's statement that she trudged everywhere on the Tube and by foot. She apparently got about London differently in the mid-1970s when he knew her. (DM)

The Green Riley

There was a touch of the 'Grand Iris' when she told me that she and a woman friend were going to tour Essex churches in a green Riley. She gave me the impression she would be driving, and seemed to be describing motoring from a more leisured age, like the thirties, when there was no traffic on the roads. I pictured the exact green of this car, not racing green but a shade of turquoise, with capaciously flared front mudguards. Query – could this trip have been with the 'Margot' in JB's books who is always rushing Iris off to see churches?

This car is a minor puzzle, like the mythical General. Your *Life* mentions a green Riley which John Bayley helped her buy in 1955, after he crashed her Hillman. But the jaunts to see churches were in the mid-'70s when it may have been put into 'honourable retirement' in the fascinating cars' graveyard at Cedar Lodge. Was the Riley of the Essex tour the same car from the '50s or – like the General – that car romantically switched to the present?

Tricks / The Invisible One

Tricks – DM: 'How did you do that?'
IM: *Oh, it's just writer's tricks.*

This time, not a trick but a clue to 'locate' the writer in a piece of writing:

IM: *The writer is always the most invisible character.*

A later note deals with Iris herself being invisibly present in this way.

The Person from Manchester

The mythic figure wasn't just someone she imagined. She

actually experienced people as mythic. A couple of examples: she told me how she had been on the interview panel to appoint Christopher Cornford's successor as Dean at the RCA. I asked her what the candidates were like, and she described *a powerful person from Manchester whom we did not appoint*. She spoke of him as if she was referring to the 'Person from Porlock' – he had become instantly mythic. But at the same time, she clearly disapproved of the sort of god-figure the poor chap had been elevated to in her mind's eye and voted against him. Nobody could be ordinary to her. As another tiny example, I remember her asking me how my brothers thought of me. Did they see me as a 'mad sage'? In fact I think they just saw me as the casualty of the family.

Persona Non Grata

She had staggered me when the job was advertised by saying, *Why don't you apply?* This was in the same category as her earlier '*Did you know Dylan?*' showing a completely gaga cognisance of the facts. I was twenty years too young to have met Dylan Thomas and the RCA would have run a mile rather than short-list me. I made Christopher Cornford distinctly anxious. He and Professor Carel Weight, both kindly men, had seen me slap my girlfriend at a private view and I had not forgotten their white faces. When I straightened myself out after leaving and began to teach, I attempted a *rapprochement* by sending Cornford, unsolicited by post, a new book on geometry that had come out (we shared this interest). It was sent back by return. I was a bull in a china shop at the RCA and, unlike the other 'working-class boys,' unpatronizable. Chatting after a group tutorial one afternoon, Cornford jokingly said, 'When David walks down the street cars get out of the way'. A kindly man, he had not meant it unkindly, but it showed how uncomfortable I made them feel – a difficult person from whom came a ripple of repulsion.

Throughout the year when IM and I overlapped, I think she stuck up for me. She was allowed to join the painting staff as an assessor at the graduation shows and argued my grade up from a Pass to 2.2. She had even held out, absurdly, for a 2.1. It should have been a Fail.

This Business of Class

In earlier letters to you, I went along with the fiction that I was working class because it fitted the plot. In fact, my background was similar to IM's – middle to lower-middle, if having parson grandfathers and bank-managers and headmistresses as aunts and uncles on my father's side makes one middle class. Even our fathers' jobs were similar: hers a census clerk, mine an insurance clerk. Also, like hers, my family lived in a closed world without friends, surrounded by books. The only difference was that hers was a happy one, containing three loving people; mine was unhappy, full of the rowing of two parents who didn't get on.

At the time I didn't resent her coming across as grand. I thought she *was* grand. I had read the 'Anglo-Irish gentry' blurb on her book jackets. The revelation that a lot of this was self-invented came as a shock. I realise now that we both created backgrounds for ourselves. Her plantation squires were mirrored by persistent myth-making by the female members in my mother's family about links with Leicestershire gentry, which I didn't entirely pooh-pooh.

I asked her as (so I thought) genuine gentry herself, whether she thought they were just tall stories. Hilariously, knowing what I now know, she weighed the pros and cons and came gravely to the conclusion that they *were*. Of the two of us, perhaps I was the more self-admitted snob – deep down I knew my stuff was made up. Did she half-sense hers was? Perhaps the fact that we shared the same fictions and had created them for the same reason – she because she was a poor girl in a rich girls' school, me because of my degradation in Birmingham and lack of education – created a bond. It is odd that somebody who warned against myth as the 'great temptation' should have been so vulnerable to her own.

Landladies

Something else that linked us (if not socially then at least antisocially) came as a surprise when I read it. It was that we had both been kicked out of a succession of digs by landladies. In my case it was understandable; I was surly and uncommunicative, and with my hospital haircut I naturally made them nervous. But I am puzzled why the young IM, so friendly and outgoing before the famous reserve set in (but perhaps a bit grand even then), should have made alarm-bells ring. A string of Birmingham women had stood on their doorsteps as I dragged my suitcase back down their garden paths, telling me I'd come to no good. But I only unnerved them; in IM's case – like the landlady in King Edward's Road, Oxford[54] – she actually seems to have been embattled with them. I can only wonder, irreverently, if it was because she brought men back.

The Irishness of Iris

Now I know she wasn't Irish, I've re-thought her Irishness and still find her very Irish. Even though I know she was just taking on the colour of a believed native land – just as she took on the colour of a believed social class – both were convincing. Not only did she think of herself as Irish, but there was a genuine touch of the 'old Irish' about her. I never heard the Irish accent everybody, including Iris, went on about. But she was convincingly Irish in her magical thinking, in her way with words, her sense of the miraculous, love of intrigue, quickness to be insulted, willingness for a fight, liking for a drink and – let's face it (I have to) –

[54] See *IMAL*, p. 317.

blarney. You could even say she was Irish in the twists and turns of her plots – like Celtic knots.

She was of course un-Irish in her famous reserve and her awkwardness in some social situations (like answering the phone!). And the Old Irish ran counter to the Scots Puritan and Wise Woman – her other two personae.

Nobody is Average to Iris

She couldn't see anybody as average. She referred to the RCA men I had brought to her party – with what I can only describe as a reverential intake of breath – as 'such good-looking boys', and was particularly taken with the rather piggy one I suspected of stealing her personalised bottle of whisky. She referred several times to my *singularly good-looking head.* The same applied to girls. I think you refer in your book to poor Carolyn, who committed suicide, being described by Iris as *beautiful*, but by others as plain and mousey. Everybody was also talented to this dear woman. I, for example (until I showed her my concrete poetry in that churchyard in Soho), was *a considerable poet; I could write like an angel*; had *improved* several bits of the Welsh medieval epic, *The Mabinogian*; was *the most audible person* from whom she had received a letter. And to cap it all, had been told, *What geniuses we both are!*

Except Paulette

There was one exception to her over-generosity about other people's looks and talents. When she had eventually met the two women in my life, meetings which she herself set up, Magda was *beautiful* or even *so beautiful*, but Paulette was *interesting*. Paulette was also *in pretty poor condition, poor child*. This may not have been disconnected with the fact that Paulette had 'jumped' Iris at the Royal College and pulled her hair. IM's disenchantment with the RCA because of the out-of-control behaviour of staff, which you mention, wasn't therefore just based on *men* being violent.

Paulette on the Warpath

Something as shocking as Paulette's attack on Iris needs a longer note. I remember it in slow motion in terms of heads rather than bodies. Iris was walking down the top corridor of the Painting School in the old Exhibition Road building, studying work at an end-of-year Show, circa 1965. Suddenly, a cloud of blonde hair detached itself from the crowds and raced the length of the corridor towards her – specifically towards the back of Iris's bobbed hair-do, which began to look increasingly vulnerable. The moment before they collided, a hand shot out of the blonde cloud and grabbed the back of the bobbed hair and pulled. A voice out of the cloud hissed, 'You and your five-pound notes'[55] and the cloud resolved itself into an incandescent and perspiring Paulette. She had landed squarely on Iris's back, nearly knocking her over, but Iris was sturdy enough to stay on her feet and took it calmly, merely muttering something about *Good luck to you*. She then made herself scarce while Paulette, intent on having it out with her at more length, roamed the building looking for her. Readers who see IM as an institution will be shocked to see her getting dragged into an affront like this. But the introduction warned that these notes would read, now and again, in fact quite a lot, as lèse-majesté. One needs to remember that the '60s was a crazy time. All of us, including Iris, were light-headed, and something as spontaneous as a famous novelist and an enraged art student rushing to collide like this could easily happen. And remember that she had deliberately exposed herself to the RCA, knowing there would be a certain amount of non-Oxfordian cut and thrust. She

55 I should add that I was at that time sponging off women in general, including Paulette, and she clearly felt that the occasional pound she scraped together for me, leaving herself short, was being badly upstaged by Iris's fivers. (DM)

could have predicted that some of it might be physical. What she could not have predicted is that it would also expose her to laughter.

Laughing at Iris

Up to the RCA incident, Paulette has appeared as a victim in these notes, stuck on the sidelines while I went mooning after Magda or got myself dolled up to meet Iris. She had even been reduced to a sort of lay figure being passed from me to another. She couldn't do much about Magda, but at least she was off the scene, trying to get away from me. Iris, however, must have been a constant irritant. She might be twenty years older and not exactly equipped to be a seductress, but Paulette saw her turning my head with drink and flattery and handouts. She knew I would lap up the attention and was enough of a snob to be seriously seduced by her fame. She also knew I was enough of a ladies' man to try it on with her. She must have been irritated most by the way I rushed off to meetings with Iris as if I was on higher business, in much the same way I had dashed off letters to her in front of Keith. What she never knew is that what she called our '*soirées*' were devoted more to Iris trying to help than seduce me. What she also suspected – and got right – was that in the early stages a lot of this help consisted of Iris trying to act as a peacemaker between me and Magda, with advice on how to get her back. So in this sense they were against Paulette and her interests.

She began to hit back and emerged as a stronger and stronger figure. Not being a girl to mess about, she began with the frontal assault described above, but soon settled for subtler methods. She chose comedy and began a concerted campaign to make Iris look ridiculous in my eyes. Magda's attitude to Iris had been wary respect; Paulette's was irreverence verging on mockery. She was completely unrepentant about the RCA incident, but however shocked

I had been I gradually found myself starting to admire the way she had taken on Iris as a rival and tried to see her off.

She found what she called 'the cherry blouse' that Iris wore at our early meetings particularly funny, and she drew cartoons of Iris *en blouse*, emphasising her dumpy body and pudding-basin haircut with me as a gawky figure at her side. There may even have been bits of paper inscribed '£5' circling in the air between us. They were screamingly funny, and to impress on me how accurate they were, she called them *photographic drawings*. The fact that she knew about the cherry blouse at all means Iris's jibe about me being a blabbermouth was all too accurate, and I had clearly been reporting things back to Paulette.

One day, on a trip out of London, walking along the Oxford Canal with Paulette, I steered us, out of curiosity, in the direction of Steeple Aston (or Paulette steered us with devilment in mind). When we got to Cedar Lodge she stood in the entrance to the drive with her hands on her hips in a sort of battle stance and began to dance with writhing movements. At the end of the drive I glimpsed a lovely ivy-covered house, not the ruin people describe. I only got a quick glimpse in the fraction of a second it took me to drag Paulette away – and it was a pretty frantic second – but nobody seemed to be in; maybe Iris was in London. If she had been in, I think I would have felt her gaze sweeping back down the drive towards us. It was hard to know whether it would have been kindly or enraged.

What I did feel though, and felt acutely, even though she might not be there, was that I had entered her domain. At St Cuthbert's I had seen *her* entering Father Irvine's domain and I have described the shiver that went through her. Now the shiver went through me, and it wasn't just a shiver in case she'd seen us.

Bit by bit Paulette worked away at my awe of Iris, and bit by bit she succeeded. Iris might still be able to inspire panic at the Oxford end on her own ground, but in London we had crossed a point at which I found her less terrifying, and something I am ashamed of happened – I let Paulette egg me on into laughing at her. I could say in defence that Iris *was* funny. She pushed earnestness to the point where it became comic. Sometimes, out of sheer relief from the seriousness of an encounter with her, one reacted by retrospective laughter. What Paulette managed to do was undermine my awe for Iris to the point where I still revered her, but at the same time could see her as faintly ridiculous, and could see that she might be faintly ridiculous in other people's eyes. It affected even the way I saw her arrive at Paddington. In the old days, she had arrived with an air of bravura as she got off the train and marched towards the barrier – a serious figure with people to meet, missions to accomplish. The same figure still arrived and it headed off into the crowds with the same determination, but there was an air of caricature about it.

Just as I accuse Iris and John Bayley of a sort of silliness *à deux*, so Paulette and I had got into a sort of mockery *à deux* – mockery of everybody. I wince at this including Iris Murdoch, but it did. From this point also, I think, dates my gradual recognition of her not just as faintly comic but also as vulnerable, which she was increasingly to become over the next fifteen years. This was a serious turning point – as serious as the point when one 'sees through a parent' for the first time and at some deep level can never feel safe again.

Then something happened in which she was to play a part with all her old power intact. One last time she would enter my life, and in the old ambivalent way – trying on one hand to calm a situation but on the other hand to stir and join it. In some ways this was to be the *tour de force* of these complicated feelings of hers, and I had never felt her so strangely and terribly present. When this thing happened P was to find her less amusing and to be very grateful for her help.

Abortion

What I didn't mention when you were preparing your book,

but which could have been mentioned because you include such an account, is that she tried to help me in a similar situation. Paulette became pregnant. When I told IM we couldn't go through with it she helped to arrange an abortion with a gynaecologist off Wimpole Street, which she would have paid for. In our case, she approached it in the same sombre manner as she did in the case of the girl civil-servant you describe in your *Life . . .* when she took upon herself 'the whole misery of the situation'.[56]

Paulette went to be examined. I was surprised by the poshness of the address but also the dustiness of the waiting room and the threadbare couch the doctor examined her on. I felt that Paulette and I had wandered, as if we were in a dream, into a scene in one of IM's novels. The couch, the dust, the faded gentility, the sun beating down on the empty street outside – the empty *back street* outside – were how one would *read* about a girl going for an abortion, not encounter it. I had the experience a second time when I went into a tiny solicitor's office in Clapham Junction and saw a clerk perched on a high stool surrounded by mountains of dusty papers – *straight out of Dickens*. Our experience in that little street was *straight out of Murdoch.*

Eventually, Paulette's own doctor capitulated and she had a NHS termination.

I have wondered about IM's motives. She saw two art students with no money, unable to cope, and tried to help them. Once again – but this time most strongly of all – I sensed that far from being outside the situation, she was watching intently from the wings, wanting to step in and even that she had created the situation – created *us* – with this possibility in mind.

56 Conradi describes how 'on one occasion Iris helped an impoverished, distressed civil service friend to have an unwanted pregnancy safely terminated, a common enough wartime scenario. The girl expressed lifelong gratitude towards Iris, who had "taken upon herself the whole misery of the situation"' (*IMA L*, p.167).

I'm not suggesting she was doing anything daft like hiding round the corner, but what I am saying, and it will sound slanderous, is that this strange woman had, out of compassion, not only taken on the misery, but also *thrilled* to it vicariously, as she had thrilled in earlier situations with my girlfriends. The abortion took this to a new level though. Paulette's pregnancy went far beyond my 'treatment of my girlfriends' in its potential for excitement. It had the potential for a much darker kind of vicarious adventure.

How – so unworldly – was she so efficient at arranging an abortion? How did she know about the Jewish doctor? Had she asked a circle of women friends? Or had she, in fact, recommended other friends in trouble to this woman? An obvious question, and not a prurient one, is how, through all her promiscuity in the 1940s, had she avoided pregnancy? Both sexes were then more naïve about contraception. Is it possible that she herself went through the devastating experience of an abortion? Is it even possible that the old doctor had been Iris's doctor? No – I must be wrong. Your *Life* confirms that she was *au fait* and gave contraceptive advice to her girlfriends.

Eclipse

Slowly Magda became a mythical figure. Paulette became the flesh and blood figure in my life, working away without recognition at the harder job of painting pictures, which she built up dot by dot. Realising the power of myth, she worked away just as patiently at blotting out Magda. She had already dealt with Iris using ridicule; now she relied on time, with its accumulation of little things we did together, to blot out the things I had done with Magda, and eventually to blot her out. Which it did – almost.

Magda faded like the Cheshire Cat in an on and off way. If you can imagine a Cheshire Cat whose appearances get less and less frequent but when they come can cause one to burst into tears. I had to endure this face grinning at me luminously over the years until Paulette produced a second face – just as luminous – my daughter's. And by a piece of good luck it fitted exactly over the other.

Swimming and the Life-Mask

DM: 'Are you a good swimmer? I'm terrified of suffocation.'
IM: *I'm a good swimmer but oddly I'm afraid of suffocation. I was nearly strangled by the umbilical cord when being born, and perhaps remember that. So I'm not sure about you doing a life-mask of me.*[57]

I had suggested she let me cast her face in plaster of Paris – I had already made one of Magda, but that casting enterprise had ended badly because she had seen it as a way to possess her and hacked it to bits. I don't think IM had qualms about being made into a trophy; she was just afraid of not being able to breathe.

Again – referring to an image of Iris:

DM: 'Could I have a photo of you?'
IM: *People sometimes photograph me but I never bother to get copies.*

I asked her for a photograph several times over the years and my early letters go on about one of her with a white cat. She never sent me one. I still wish I'd taken a camera to one of our meetings, particularly one of the last ones, and clicked us both at arms length, but I left it too late and probably wouldn't have dared. When I told you how much I regretted this, you said, 'She'd have loved it'.

[57] This may throw some light on Rene Murdoch exclaiming, when asked if she thought Iris would ever have children, 'I jolly well hope not!' and confirms John Bayley's theory that the birth had been traumatic. (DM)

When I tried to make that cast back in 1965, it had been trophy-hunting pure and simple – to put her face on the wall, the way I had added her name to the list of girls.

A Dark Place

It would give these notes an elegiac ring to say I wanted to photograph her to eternalise her, because she was slipping away. The signs were there and I had begun to spot them. I have described the confused goodbye on the platform at Paddington after our Bizarro Restaurant meeting. We were both flustered and banging into each other and she was more dazed than I had ever seen her, which had been one of the reasons for the confusion. This was followed by the meeting at the Stanhope which she forgot to turn up for, and by now I was certain something was wrong. I suspected it might be dementia and, if it was, she wouldn't just be slipping, she would soon be crashing into that ocean she had described herself falling into, as the way she went to sleep. But I still had so much invested in her that I pretended it was absent-mindedness.

Someone, somewhere in your *Life*, remarks that even when she was young she was often 'somewhere else' and I felt this too. She was often 'rapt,' and her 'raptness' did disguise the onset of Alzheimer's very subtly and cruelly. I don't mean she was 'away with the fairies' in some fey Irish way, but that she was always at a remove, and this could imitate the fugues of the genuinely simple. To get through she had to put her head down and charge. And she did get through. When I sat next to her in a pub and our foreheads bumped accidentally, I felt hers blundering towards me in an effort to engage, and it engaged wonderfully. But when our heads blundered together again at Paddington at our last meeting, hers was just bedraggled and anxious.

You were all filled with pity; I was filled with a mixture of pity and irritation. My real feeling, after waiting an hour and a half outside the Stanhope in Gloucester Road for nothing, had been irritation that she could be so gaga. I couldn't enter into the misery of it. I wanted to grab her and shake her out of it. You must remember what she used to be to me. She had been infallible: she had *been* everything, *known* everything, *put me right* about everything and, however big the gap between meetings got, I always knew she was there, *compos mentis*, ready to come to the rescue.

She might have become hesitant; I might have begun to see through her; I might have seen her momentarily as a caricature; but deep down the old awe was still there. And this had been proved by the way I'd imagined her gaze sweeping down the drive at Cedar Lodge – the gaze of somebody still very much all there. It was essential she remained all there. An Iris Murdoch not all there was unthinkable. Even though I must have been in my fifties by then, it made me feel insecure.

So my initial reaction to her Alzheimer's was a brutal refusal to believe in it. I blanked out pitiable things. One was the way her head changed. Over the last few meetings I saw it gradually change from the ragged page-boy head of the middle-aged novelist into what at first sight looked like the same head, but a heavier version of it. It puzzled things out as hard as ever and nodded wisely in the old way, but a struggle was going on and it seemed to be overdoing the erudition, giving it the air of an *idiot savant*. Its hair, instead of looking as if it had been cut by John Bayley with erratic scissors, as it usually did, looked increasingly as if it had been cut by an institution. I couldn't help remembering the women in Rubery with their pinafores and cropped heads.

Re-reading this, it sounds brutal and overwritten – a morbid exaggeration of signs other people would have missed. Can I really have seen her like this as early as 1995? And how can somebody who says he loved her, talk about 'its' head, not 'her' head?

I think the answer has to be that I had not only blanked

her out because I felt I was being dropped, but had to some extent fallen out of love with her. My first reaction to her Alzheimer's was this refusal to believe it was happening. Then, when I realised what it was, I experienced a mixture of feelings: one short-lived moment of real grief; a moment of panic that now her mind wasn't there – *she* wasn't there and I was on my own; a re-experiencing of my terrors at seventeen of brain-cells being blacked out (by ECT)[58] and a monstrously selfish regret that I was disappearing from her neurones until they would no longer contain me. These are the things I think I felt. But perhaps brutality was the only alternative to sympathy. A single attempt to imagine sympathetically what was going on inside her head was enough to unhinge one's own mind.

I am still puzzled why I was not more upset. Perhaps we had become more estranged than I realised. Perhaps these notes make us sound closer than we were. We weren't even friends in a normal sense. We were just two people who had met accidentally when my head came round her door; who had experienced a momentary epiphany or 'recognition' or 'click' – whatever you want to call it – and then got stuck in this peculiar admonishing relationship. Despite the 'letting go' early on, my various mistakes over the years had put us on the more formal footing I have described. In the end, meetings were events I had to pluck up courage for and, as she became frailer, perhaps they were for her too.

You and John Bayley and her inner circle felt the full pity of what was happening (to the point where, I believe, it still pains you so much you can only refer to it in a hushed way). You were all much closer than I was. She was still a force in my life but a more abstract one. She had turned into what I can only describe as a sort of sacred monster to whom something monstrous was happening, remote from me, in Oxford.

'Sacred monster!' you will exclaim. 'What an impossible

[58] Electro-Convulsive Therapy. (DM)

term to apply to Iris'. One could call Canetti a sacred monster – didn't John Bayley call him the 'god monster' of Hampstead? But Iris had always been the acolyte of such creatures, drawn by their auras, too gentle ever to become one herself no matter what awe one held her in. And when she metamorphosed them into the central figures in her books, she had told me that the writer (herself), if present at all as a character, was always on the edge. Now, by a paradox – horrible to her friends but in a way also wonderful – Alzheimer's had made Iris herself mythic. Not by becoming stronger but by being struck down by innocence, she had moved from the edge to the centre, surrounded by her attendant figures – John Bayley, you, Jim and the Friends, in whom she inspired not awe but love.

This is what it felt like to me in London, imagining the scene in Oxford. It can't have felt much like this to you and the others experiencing the day-to-day job of looking after her. John's book, with its true picture of what was happening at Charlbury Road, hadn't, of course, been written. I next imagined a sort of radiant child with all of you around her. I tried to imagine more exactly what this Child looked like, by projecting myself like a floating eye to Oxford and looking over your shoulders. Was she in fact radiant, or was this just schmalz? I didn't know what Alzheimer's did to people; I morbidly imagined that the nodding head I remembered from our last pub meetings might have become enormous, really turning her into monster, and the morbid image would have been reinforced if I had known about the mess, the bids to escape from the house, the animal noises or the odd outbursts of rage. But between the troubled intervals, you mention outbursts of love, and when I read this and saw the late photographs in your book, the monstrous image that had been troubling me dissolved, and I was left with just the sacred part of it. You describe her as sanctified by simplicity, as kissing people's hands and bowing. What you don't describe, perhaps because you hadn't felt it in the same oddly persistent way

I had, was whether by becoming simple she had also lost the mysterious sexuality that I have hinted at in so many of my notes about her.

She was now out of my life, and anyway it was all happening in Oxford – at HQ – far away from the riffraff of her more picaresque London chums, like me. But I had felt the full rush of her love for two years at the age of twenty-four, had felt it twiddle my hair that night on Tamworth Station, and she had stubbornly gone on loving me, at least at half-strength, for thirty years. I was tempted a couple of times to get on the train and go and ring the bell at Charlbury Road, but I felt the inner circle had closed round her and I was now so on the fringe it would have been cheek. And by 1998 she wouldn't have known me anyway.

Postscript

Inevitably, now she's dead and we have discovered there were so many of us, the people she knew try to work out where we stood in the pecking order of her affections and what she saw us *as*. You said in a TV programme after her death that 'she liked monsters – male and female'.[59] I have to face the fact that as well as being a casualty I was probably also a monster, although not on the scale of Canetti and certainly not a 'sacred' one in the sense he was, or she (for me) so strangely became because of the monstrousness of Alzheimer's.

In some ways it was flattering to be a monster. You couldn't quite believe you *were* one but why fight it? From being a nobody you found yourself elevated, in her eyes at least, to the role of an archetype, putting you on a par with beings like the Minotaur. You were suddenly interesting. And if you were lucky you might even get into one of her books as a character, even if you had to face the fact that top monsters like Canetti outshone you in horribleness and would always get the best parts.

The older, more-established monsters among her friends probably didn't even realise they were monsters and just went on being gloriously themselves, secure in her love. But I suspect the younger, more-nervous ones like me had that feeling I have already described – that we might have made it as figures in her personal mythos, but we were still on the fringe and were never going to make it into the circle

59 *Iris Murdoch, Strange Love* (Omnibus, BBC 1, 2002)

of the most loved, like John Bayley and Steiner and some of the people she dedicated her books to. We had each been briefly at the centre during that 'moment of recognition' that began each of her friendships, when it had been excitingly just us and her. Now our job was to stand as a ring of strange creatures just outside it and be ready for her to make an occasional dash from the centre to make sure we were OK and perhaps to run her fingers through our hair.

We felt loved, but loved as what? When the fun of being a monster wore off we just wanted to be known as ourselves, and felt a monster role had been forced on us. In my case, that it was something I had pretended to be a bit too convincingly and been stuck with. It never occurred to us, because we couldn't face our own awfulness, that this is what we really were and she was loving us AS ourselves. So we are left a bit in limbo about who, and what, we were to her.

Her own attitude to her monsters was ambivalent. She felt bound to reform them but couldn't stop loving their awfulness. Nothing, for example, could have been more down-to-earth than the way she went on at me to behave better: it was addressed very directly to me as ME. But when I was away from her I sometimes wondered: was I David? Or was she stretching out her hand to stroke a horn on my forehead like the Lady in *The Lady and the Unicorn* tapestries she loved so much and sent me a postcard of. I never knew – and perhaps neither did she – whether it was to stroke a horn on my forehead or to turn me into a human being.

I'd like to be able to say that it was the latter and that she humanised me, and as you do in your book that, 'soon he was a college lecturer living by some of the values her loving but admonishing letters (and conversations) tried to instil'. And to echo the others who say she was transformative in their lives. I'm surprised not to have been changed more. You would think such absolute goodness was bound to change everything it touched. So I'd like to say she changed my life, and these notes suggest that she did. But of course she didn't. I wasn't changed by Iris; I was changed by my

Birmingham experiences, which temporarily humanised me and made me a *mensch*.[60] And later, when that had worn off, I was changed by just the plain necessity of holding down a job and at least *acting* as a decent father. What she does, though, is to work on me as a constant voice of correction – a series of affectionate tickings-off – *Come on David; Come off it David* – which I half-listen to and, now and again, half-act on.

But one needs to conserve one's wickedness as well as one's goodness, and deep down I go on in the same old solipsistic way. I'm basically still bone-idle, still revengeful. I still ride rough-shod over women, if they'll let me. I'm still wrapped up in the past; still hang on like grim death to the present. I still won't let go of people who should be let go of, and there is a danger that the dedicatee of these notes may replace Magda in that role, with no Iris to argue that she be set free. Worst of all, I am now beginning to experience funk – pure blind funk – in the face of something new. The voice will have to say 'be brave' where that is concerned, and say it pretty firmly. Is it conceivable she could even help one get through *that*?

She is a woman I have begun to forget. She belongs to a grand period of my life when I was young, experiencing the tears of the youth of all the world, with Paulette, Magda and Keith – who almost certainly didn't experience it. Because the whole point of being young is that you don't know you're young. You can't – mustn't – see yourself *sub specie aeternitatis* – it has to be done blindly. So they just got on with it, and got through it, and probably haven't given it a thought for thirty years.

The 1960s and '70s were the heyday of the people in these notes, and it was her heyday before her books got too long and her reputation began to wobble. I'm just grateful, for whatever reason – compassion, curiosity, or simply the urge to join in – that she did so, and took the plunge.

60 Yiddish/German word meaning a decent, honourable man.

'You capture things no one else has' – Peter Conradi's closing letter to David Morgan

Dear David,

I read this and think it wonderful. You capture things no-one else has. For example how alarming she could be. And how much complexity underlay the outward simplicity she had achieved.

Your book also touches on a delicate and interesting question that she repeatedly addressed in her Gifford lectures in my hearing in 1982, but which I think may be missing or under-stated when she came to write these lectures up as *Metaphysics as a Guide to Morals.* She took the view that *even the most virtuous apprehension of another human being need not necessarily exclude an erotic element.* This, I remember her repeating, could quietly co-exist with other elements within a friendship. She believed that this erotic element could be implicit rather than explicit and, if expressed at all, should be so only up to defined limits, one primary duty of the good moral agent being to sublimate 'low Eros'. A difficult feat, one extremely liable to misunderstanding or misrepresentation by outsiders – but one she had the courage to learn to carry out. And you show this, too.

Perhaps you underestimate, at least in my view, the extent to which ALL her friends were compartmentalised, and hence might be said to have experienced themselves as 'outsiders', partly due to her 'pudeur' (modestly, inwardness, secrecy, shyness). This only dissolved for me from 1996 on, when the tasks entailed in looking after many of her needs – including bathing her and washing her hair – fell increasingly to Jim and me.

You uniquely – and believably – capture her ability to love others unselfishly, and for this all her friends and admirers will owe you a continuing debt.

Best,
Peter

With Love and Rage in Context

The Centre for Iris Murdoch Studies, Kingston University

The Centre for Iris Murdoch Studies was inaugurated in 2004 when it acquired two important archives to add to its existing extensive Murdoch collections. The first is Iris Murdoch's working annotated library of over 1,000 books, which she kept at her Oxford home and which ranges through published works on philosophy, psychology, poetry, literature, art and travel. The annotations in many of the books are of significant scholarly interest, potentially providing years of analysis and work for researchers. The second is the working archive of Peter Conradi, Iris Murdoch's authorized Biographer, and comprises correspondence (including a series of holograph letters), typescripts (including an unpublished book on Heidegger), interviews, transcripts and cassettes. Since 2004 the Centre has acquired other important archive materials and letter-runs relating to Murdoch's life and work. They include letters from Murdoch to her friend, the painter Barbara Dorf, to the writers Roly Cochrane and Scott Dunbar and to her Oxford contemporary and life-long friend, Denis Paul. Many hundreds of letters have been acquired in total. Thus the Centre for Iris Murdoch Studies now offers fresh biographical information and primary source material for researchers worldwide who are developing new readings of Murdoch's novels and seeking to track her intellectual development in relation to specific aspects of her philosophy, theology and moral psychology. Kingston University and the Iris Murdoch Society continue to support the expansion of the archives and the University now employs a full-time archivist to look after its important special collections.

The donation of any materials relating to Iris Murdoch would be greatly appreciated. We also welcome financial assistance that would enable the Iris Murdoch Society to contribute to the purchase of important archival material that may come on to the market in the future. Those who would like to contribute financially, donate letters or other memorabilia, or record their memories of Iris Murdoch, should contact: Dr Anne Rowe, the Director of the Centre for Iris Murdoch Studies, Kingston University, Penrhyn Road, Kingston, Surrey, KT1 2EE, Tel: +44 (0)20 8417 7012, Email: a.rowe@kingston.ac.uk

Facsimile copies of letters and poems

The sum of daylight is the moon's revenge
You wait for manoeuvres to eschew the end
Ah hopefully you leave the moment's garden
Asking the flowers to absolve that scorn.
Sweet day's attendant, you are not without
The tears of tribute to a vanished dew—
The salt of seas that never knew a day
Or caves where dead seals suffocated lie

[illegible]

Moonboots of shadow
the misfit drags.
Pieces of street not made to
fit at midnight on mosaic;
Instead they pass lugubriously
down pavements lit by gas,
Limpingly,
With the long lope of the insane.

For this man is mad;
The last time I saw his feet
Was somewhere on the Road
to Tarascon
In broad daylight,
Weighed down not just with boots
of shade
But with a whole landscape
He dragged behind him.

DM

Yes, you are a
wolf, & have sent me
a very wolfish letter, full

closer — and perhaps it's
surprising that we held on
so long with only Piero
della Francesca between
us like a drawn sword. Well,

splendid to see you. I
do love you. Thank you
for showing me the
bell — that was
wonderful! Some god

Did you receive
from me (a) a cheque,
(b) a cake? You
don't mention either

to it. I was feeling
so tired yesterday,
but simply touching
you made the tiredness
go away. I was so

careful not to go too far. I sometimes want to cause you "pain" but never pain. That is, it must be contained within love. But you understand

I am worried about what seems to me your tendency to romanticise M_ & all this talk about cutting people up. This seems to me, besides being morally wrong, a sheer failure of intelligence on your part, something dull & blunting in your mind, something that makes you "captive".

I think you bring out in me (tutor here rather than aunt) a streak of mild sadism.

perhaps it is as well that you should know I can be angry.

my dear boy, I'm very sorry
to hear about these
intolerable hiccups. (You

a proper way
'gruff & neuter' persona,
you must keep in mind
that I have behind me
25 years of being told in
the most extravagant
terms that I am beautiful.

Know, I know, about
being viciously in love,
and I have pursued
~~people~~ long and with
ingenuity, but never with
your relentlessness in the
face of a refusal. I have
also been relentlessly pursued
& have hated the pursuer —
& then when I wearied him
out felt sorry. I think
you must somewhere ~~[illegible]~~
in your mind locate the
possibility of total failure
here —

Letters

A note on the full-length letters

As the title *With Love and Rage* and the Introduction make clear, my friendship with IM, and the letters that trace it, switched in tone between affection and anger. Many of the italics quotes in the text were chosen to show this, but my editors felt it would be a good idea to authenticate these by including the complete text of a few letters. Like the extracts, these divide quite dramatically into two kinds – into letters to somebody she loved, but also to somebody who could make her very angry. And she pulls no punches in either direction – the affection or the anger doesn't come in flashes, but is kept up over eight or nine pages.

LOVE

Letter 1
Date: 20th June 1964

This letter marks our discovery and recognition of each other at our first meeting away from the RCA, at Harcourt Terrace and the dropping of formality. I had written to her with confused feel - ings after the meeting and this is her reply, reassuring me and declaring her own feelings. Her longest letter to me.

Dear David,
Thank you very much for your letter/ Yes, I think maybe I have underestimated your common-sense. Perhaps in a way even underestimated you. On Thursday & Friday (hence my card from Cambridge) I began to wonder whether you were not by now seeing Wednesday evening as a dream or feeling alarmed or baffled by it - & whether you might not feel it beyond your ingenuity to know how to write to me. In fact you have known very well how to write; and I am impressed by your immediate ability to be, as it were, 'tough' with me. I don't mean that I expected you to be awed or flattered (I equally expected you to be resentful) – but I am pleased by the way you at once treat with me as one sovereign state treating with another. This is nothing but good.

I had intended, earlier, that we should part for the vacation on rather more formal terms. But by last Wednesday it had become impossible not to touch you & to draw you a good deal closer – and perhaps it's surprising we held out so long with only Piero della Francesca between us like a drawn sword. Well, no, not surprising – maybe it couldn't have happened earlier though it had to happen then. About the vacation – I'm not being masochistic in saying 'till October', nor am I wanting to make you into a 'medallion' (I'll talk about that in a minute) – I just didn't want us both to be troubled by perhaps brief & isolated meetings (where someone might say something which would be misunderstood, or where something might go wrong which couldn't then be put right face to face.) I have a hell of a lot of work to do this summer – and while I wanted somehow to 'secure' things before we parted I didn't want to be in a state of being irrationally upset by you or about you during the interval. (straightforward self-interest.) In fact things have moved more swiftly & also our ability to understand each other seems greater that I expected – although in many ways, & in spite of all your talk. I still don't altogether know what goes on inside that singularly good-looking head of yours. I'd like to see you sooner too, but let us leave it at 'October' & not worry about it for the present.

I would like to take away your suspicions & mistrusts, but perhaps only time & experience can altogether do that. I do want to know you and love you wholeheartedly, as one entire person dealing with another. And I want this to be 'clean-cut': I too have had so many muddled & twisted relationships, and I want ours to be steady & clear, & I think it can be. (I have, by the way, mentioned your existence in general terms to John Bayley, who trusts me absolutely & never wants to hear details. All that side of things is OK. I was touched and pleased that it occurred to you.)

I was very glad that you used the words 'safe' and 'secure' – I did want to communicate this to you & hope I've really succeeded. I think you must really know that I'm not collecting you like a 'medallion' or treating you like a 'young man', in the peculiar sense you attach to this, & you must know by now that I am not keeping 'the saner part of my mind' untouched by this. I am all here.

Apropos the 'young man' question: you are, as you observed, not all that young – and of course I don't feel myself to be all that old. You may believe I am 44, but I don't. Yet of course in other ways, I do apprehend you as splendidly young, often as something like a son or a child, and I shall never stop regarding you as my pupil. (You may suffer from this from time to time.)

The enclosed is payment for painting or paintings to be specified later. If anyone else wants to buy paintings, for God's sake sell them. There will always be plenty for me. If you are later in a financial fix please let me know – by the method you suggested or any other method. I am glad you feel you can go on painting this summer. I look forward to seeing the 96 drawings. And I very much want to see you using colour and using the stuff which was (I must admit I thought rather enchantingly) entangled in your hair on Wednesday. Also for Christ's sake think soberly about the job question. In about a month I shall want a report from you on what you've done about it. And you must act sooner rather than later, or jobs will be filled. I am hoping you will show unexpected common sense here.

And don't get yourself into trouble. The revenge fantasies you spoke of have nothing to do with 'virility' or 'manhood' in any admirable sense, but are connected with what's muddled & muddy in you, & represent everything that will hinder your attempt to resemble Piero. I've thought a lot about X, but I don't know enough about the situation to have any wisdom. She may well feel 'hunted' or indeed 'haunted' by you at present.

I haven't got a copy of the photo with the white cat, but I'll try to get one. (It's not my favourite photograph of myself.) I will also send you a scarf, but not yet. And I will later on ask you for the piece of the life mask.*

I must stop this letter now: I won't normally write you long ones. (By the way, you won't get put into the workshop. I understand all that.)

I hope the address I've put on the envelope is OK? Let me now if not. Write when you feel like it, before long. I may not reply instantly but, unless I'm away (&I'll let you know about that) I'll reply within 2 or 3 days. I hoped that before term ended I could convey to you some sense of security. What I didn't expect was that you would succeed in conveying a sense of security to me, but I think you have done that. I am very glad that you exist. Do think seriously about jobs & work well.

Ever, IM

PS. I think the painter we were trying to remember who did the luminous profile portrait in the National Gallery is Baldovinetti – I don't otherwise know him, do you?

** I narcissistically cast my face in plaster and gave her a copy (DM)*

Letter 2
Date: late 1964

A short letter written when we'd each been through a bad patch (she exhausted by writing – I by a bout of despair which is made clearer in the letter that follows), but now we both feel rejuvenated. To interest her I had gone round London finding real-life motifs from her novels to show her. In this case it was a huge bell (The Bell) in a crypt at Brompton. When I told her about it, we piled into a taxi like excited children to go and see it.

My dear child, it was splendid to see you. I do love you. Thank you for showing me the bell – that was wonderful! Some god must have led you to it. I was feeling so tired yesterday, but simply touching you made the tiredness go away. I was so glad to find you (somehow and so evidently) 'whole' again. You have much health and strength in you. Please get us the Welsh record. I enclose the £2 it will probably cost. Also, do examine your financial situation and let me know if you need anything to keep you going. I hope one of the jobs materialises. In case you have any freedom in the choice of times, keep in mind that I am in London during term from Tuesday morning or afternoon till Thursday afternoon. But if you have to absent then you have to & we must think our way round that.

I want those photographs of your 'angel' some time. I'm sure you have a most remarkable painter inside you. I embrace you.

Ever, I

Letter 3
Date: 18th October 1964

A long letter on various topics and varied in tone from 'mock aunt' whom I have set out to shock to fellow artist talking about her work. Just as I have taken her to see a bell at Brompton, I take her to an exhibition at the Museum of Mankind to see severed heads apropos that novel (Severed Heads) and she is excited by them but reluctant to let me turn her into one by casting her face in plaster. She sees my room in Ladbroke Grove for the first time and scans it approvingly as the proper sort of monastic cell for an artist to work in, not realising how little art actually takes place there, (she is to be less charmed on her second visit when she discovers I am keeping copies of our letters to each other).

Steeple Aston
Dear David,
Thank you very much for your boy to aunt letter (though the later part wasn't quite suitable for an aunt.) There is that element perhaps in our curious friendship. At Bianchi's restaurant I felt a little as if I were taking somebody out from school. (That meal was lunch by the way. We are not U. enough to call it luncheon.)

Your capacity to not-write letters is about equal, but only just, to my capacity not to receive them. I meant to say to you when we met that I'd like you to write at least once a week, but I think I'll now shorten that to four days. (write oftener of course if you want to.) After four days of silence I shall start to worry about you. No need to write much if you have no words (though I can scarcely imagine you without words.) And, as I say, do write as often as you please, it couldn't be too often.

Yes, I am good swimmer. (It is in character somehow that you are not.) But I am also especially terrified of suffocation. (I was nearly strangled once by the umbilical cord when being born & perhaps 'remember' that.) So I'm not sure about the life mask trial. Do you know <u>why</u> these heads and masks interest you?

Your fellatio idea (necrofellatio) is very powerful. No, it was never in my mind. I was too dominated by the image of the head as actually used by these tribes, a very taboo object. (Also the eye to eye relation.) There was also the Medusa-genitals-sun image, but this was less important. Yes, a supreme blasphemy. You have a more blasphemous and obscene mind than I have, which could be a gift to you as an artist.

Keats and Blake , yes. And we might make that severed head tour of London, & various other ones. We obviously have different Londons. (But so has everyone.) Your Kensal Green idea was so beautiful and felicitous. I'm glad you made me wait.

I'm pleased to have seen your large cell-like room. I meant to ask you about the pictures. One clearly yours(?) The other? Don't forget you are going to frame a drawing, or drawings, for me. I so very much hope you'll find you are able to work this summer. Should you draw, paint, more from life? I seem to remember your saying you hadn't done enough of that. (Aunt touch. How various one is, what with aunts, Oscar Wilde etc. I rather like the image of myself as Oscar Wilde.)

Your criticisms, implied & otherwise, of what I write are acute & such as I would make myself. (Perhaps these two phrases mean the same.) It is a question of getting one's motive power and one's technique together. I have plenty of both, but they don't cooperate properly. One mars the other. (This isn't a strong enough image for the misery of the situation.) You are quite right that Effingham was never really in that bog. It was all intellectual. Equally, in this novel that's coming out in the autumn and that I wish you wouldn't see, somebody is supposed to be burnt to death only of course they aren't as there are no real flames. These failures which envelop and <u>are</u> one's whole being can feel crushing. The answer is not 'Joyceisation' (which would be Millerisation) but some kind of courage which I scarcely know the name of.

I'm going to Dorset tomorrow and then back to Kent (I may pass through London, but only between trains) & will be away a week or a bit less. (So the 4 day rule can be relaxed - only I'll hope for a letter waiting on my return.) There's a lot I'd like to say to you, only perhaps today I am not as well supplied with words as usual. (It's good that we are both pretty ready users of these things.) I have a very great good will towards you and your existence is a source of happiness to me. I so much hope that you'll be able to dominate, control, get through the trials of, this summer, and as it were tame and handle yourself, in a sense of 'tame' which is more like providing oneself with a steely backbone. I do hope things with X will take a sudden good turn (life is surprising) or at any rate become something you can think about sanely and without maddening pain. Don't <u>not</u> talk about it to me because you think you've talked about it too much. You haven't, and if it's uppermost in your mind you must talk about it.

I've asked Parker's bookshop in Oxford* to send you the Shakespeare I spoke of, & it should turn up in about a week, they are rather slow. Are youW.10 or W.11, by the way? You seem in doubt yourself.

Thanks for the life mask. It's a weird trophy and doesn't resemble you any more than the photo does. But I can remember your face.

Do look after yourself, David, and don't fall into despairs. You are a precious being to me.

With love to you and all hopeful wishes, I.

* *misremembered as Blackwells in the text (DM)*

Letter 4
Date: 30th June 1965

A wonderful letter of counselling and consolation regarding my relationship with --. She describes her own experiences of pursu - ing and being rejected (Canetti?) and tells me that I must let go and find some indestructible centre in myself, however small, that can survive. Looking ahead, she sees that there may be trouble from knowing m, and I have warned her of this, but she thinks the relationship is strong enough to stand any shocks.

Cedar Lodge
Steeple Aston
Oxford
June 30th
Dear David,
I was relieved to get your letter, though very sorry to hear about the X situation. I suddenly started to worry about you at the weekend, thought you mightn't have got my letter, and thought too that you might be too deep in trouble or despair to be able to write.

About X: you know you may just have to let go here. Only I know you can't envisage it. Anyway for God's sake stop the pursuit tactics. Suddenly to break off the pursuit might make her miss you. Not here today - why? I'm sure a letter suggesting a very limited time during which you would wait is the thing. Yes, I know, I know, about being insanely in love, and I have pursued people long and with ingenuity, but never with your relentlessness in the face of refusal. I have also been relentlessly pursued and have hated the pursuer - & then when I wearied him felt sorry. I think you must somewhere in your mind locate the possibility of total failure here - & with that change your tactics. I know how one feels that one person can make one be at last oneself. But there has got to be also a central point, even if it is very small, which knows it can and has got to survive in the face of anything & be indestructible. Don't find this gloomy stuff. I do hope very much for you and X (I imagine X a lot). But do change the pursuit tactics.

Listen, I would like to see you & will be in London this coming Friday, July 3rd. Could I see you at Harcourt Terrace about 6.30? I shall almost certainly get a train which gets to Paddington just before 6, and by taxi should be along by 6.30. If by any unlikely chance I miss that train, I'll be on the next train which arrives at 7, & will arrive Harcourt Terrace about 7.30. I know you've had practice in waiting, but I'd hope not to make you wait. Only (assuming you can manage Friday) don't clear off if I'm not there by half past six. I still keep this illusion that you obey me implicitly, although you've already disobeyed me once in a matter of substance!)

It's hard to say briefly what I think about a lot of the other things you have said in your letters. Of course I will talk to you about myself & not with reluctance when the time comes. But (although we don't seem to have been doing badly lately) we may not get to know each other all that quickly. This doesn't worry me, because I feel an extraordinary certainty about this thing. I am very steady in my attachments. As for your 'warnings': I do recognise you as somebody who could be a deliberate wrecker of something he valued, but I'm not afraid of this here. Perhaps I imagine that I can 'manage' you, still relying on the authority which you said failed to impress you even at our first meeting. But not just that, David. I am capable of caring for you a great deal, and that is what will have to stand whatever shocks there are. I'm not so easily jolted as your 'silver spoon' and rush-covered halls' line of talk suggests you think. Getting to know some-body involves the removal of romanticism, & there's probably a good deal be removed. (And there's suffering in this too.) But here we are, and this thing plainly demands to be thought of in terms of permanence.

Your letters are very self-giving and you-like. (Even the way you cross things out is like you, & like a painter.) Yes, I will tell you if I ever think you are being hypocritical – though this is often hard to tell – we are so mixed & blended. But what mostly strikes me about you is that you are naturally, indeed involuntarily, honest.

I won't write you short replies (unless you call this short) – except maybe if I'm just going away somewhere, in which case I'll try to reply properly soon. I wish with all my heart that I could help you about X – it's no good saying 'Don't despair' or 'Don't suffer'. I know what this pain is like.

I hope you can manage Friday evening? If I'm not there at 6.30, I'll be there at 7.30, but more likely 6.30. Keep going and don't do anything foolish. I embrace you.

Ever, IM

Letter 5
Date: 1965

This letter marks the low point in the history of her handouts to me and the lengths she went to, to help. Probably interrupting herself in the middle of writing a novel, she runs fruitlessly round Steeple Aston for money and sends me the emergency pound from her handbag.

Dear David,
I've just got back from Kent, & found a letter of yours which must date from some time ago – it was the <u>first</u> letter about the financial crisis, to which the ones I got before Christmas referred back. So I am rather confused about the situation. Could you write <u>at once</u> & let me know how things stand & what you need? I get the point about cheques being no use. The trouble is that here in deep country it is not easy to raise actual pound notes – no bank, and my post office savings account is unfortunately empty just now. Our shop will sometimes change a small cheque, but usually they have very little ready money & don't like handing it out. A ridiculous difficulty. but there it is. If necessary I will write to a

friend in London (another faithful ex-pupil) & ask her to send you some notes or postal order. And if I can raise a small sum at the village shop I will try to get it into today's post, or tomorrow's at latest. I never actually have much money with me, especially after being away, & am now down to my last ten bob.

Please write at once with general report on your welfare. Have you managed to heat your room any better? If you use a paraffin stove be careful.

There's deepish snow here & the house is frozen from end to end. Much love.

PS Forgot it's early closing day in village & haven't been able to raise any money at all. I enclose an emergency pound which I found in my handbag. You should tomorrow receive ten pounds via one of my ex-pupils. Write soon with all news. With love.

RAGE

Letter 6
Date: January 1967

My one effort to get a teaching job has ended in the sack and I am back on the dole. Her letters are still affectionate but a scathing note is creeping in – I am not looking hard enough for a job, expecting to be supported 'in literary idleness'. She has warned me in earlier letters that she might one day offer me unflattering as well as flattering pictures of myself and this is the first example. By letter 8 her disillusionment with me will be complete. In it her tone changes from mild telling-off for being lazy to the shattering accusation that I am a liar, a self-aggrandiser and 'have a kind of cruelty which she has never met before'. But she still won't abandon me.

Dear David,
Thank you for your letter. You don't give any news of P. I hope she is OK & reasonably recovered?

If I really had your interests at heart I would probably send no money. I cannot understand why you don't work part of the summer. Can't you get some sort of job? You do a very easy, as far as time goes, part-time job for half the year, & you can't complain of not having time for your own work as an artist. Why don't you do a hands turn for the human race during the summer? Or do you detest work so much? (I note that while I am working hard at Steeple Aston earning money to give you, you are enjoying yourself in the Isle of Skye, of which you dutifully write quite a nice account.) I think it is bad for you not to do at least a little ordinary work, such as ordinary people do. I hope things are otherwise all right with you.

I'm glad you saw your mother and R.

Best wishes, I

Letter 7
Date: September 1965

Her long-suffering efforts to help me get a job or a place at university via her contacts and testimonials turns to farce when I muddle the name of the man to write to and she sends him a testimonial with his name horribly misspelt. She has already suspected (unfairly) that I am muffing interviews on purpose and in this letter she explodes.

Dear David,
I'm not in much of a mood for being amused by your blunders. I dislike being made to look a fool. (Also the effect of that careful letter will be entirely spoiled.) If you haven't enough sense of accuracy (or even sense) to check the name of someone on whom your future may depend it doesn't look as if you'll get far in the academic world. Henceforth I leave you to make your own arrangements. If & when you

get a place somewhere I'm prepared to make a financial contribution – I can't say how large, since my income fluctuates considerably. Meanwhile I'd advise you to get on with the Latin, and get yourself a job that pays so that you can save some money. Best of luck.

PS I'm away now for about a week

Letter 8
Date: April 1965

This letter marks the end of the first phase of the relationship inaugurated by Letter 1. She has already said, 'It's as well you know I can be angry', and I learn how truly angry she can be in this letter. I had broken the rule of 'keep your mouth shut – be discreet' and it has terrible consequences. She freezes the corre - spondence and the relationship, but it doesn't end things.

Dear David,
I am terribly unhappy about this business, & simply cannot understand how you can have behaved as you did. I was very reluctant to believe (even when you told me yourself) that you had told deliberate lies about me of a very damaging kind. And I still thought when I last saw you in London that there had been a good deal of misunderstanding. I came back last Thursday to find a letter from X which finally convinced me that you must have lied quite deliberately and maliciously, knowing what you were doing, & that over a long time you had been intentionally poisoning his mind against me.

It is very doubtful now whether he will ever believe me or trust me

----- *deleted section* -----

I also feel a very deep and especially tormenting grief to think that somebody vulnerable and whom I like very much should have been led to think of me as a thoroughly odious and callous person.

I simply cannot understand your motives here. As you said, you certainly have an instinct to estrange people you are fond of. But it seems

you also have a kind of cruelty which I've never met before. I suggest you must have enjoyed using your power to hurt X, & using him in turn to torment me.

I'm afraid this can't be overlooked or got round, & you have destroyed an innocent & happy affection for you which I valued. I care very much for my professional scrupulousness & you could not have hurt or damaged me more vitally than in making me fail (or seem to fail) – *deleted* -- I have always been very careful as a teacher. But clearly the worst and most foolish thing I ever did was to make friends with you.

I'm not going to 'abandon' you (unless you wish it) but we must make another start on a different basis. I know I have a responsibility for this disastrous friendship & I stand by my mistakes. But you are a very dangerous person to have for a friend, & it would be very irresponsible of me (as well as psychologically impossible) to go on as before. (God knows what lies you have told about me in other quarters.) I don't want to see you at present. (I feel I would simply have nothing to say to you.) There had better be an interval during which the impression left by this wretched business can fade a little. I will send you a note in the second half of term & will see you then, if you want to see me.

In the meantime write if you want to and I will reply. (I note that you had the insolence to keep a carbon copy of a letter to me & show it to someone else.) If you could now tell X the whole truth & make him understand that I did not make the detestable remarks you attributed to me, that would be of some service – though I expect by now he does not believe a word you say.

I think there is nothing else you can say to either of us except that you are very sorry for what you have done, which I hope you are. I wish you well.

PS I am sorry to write you this disagreeable letter and to cause you pain. I am utterly miserable about the whole thing

Letter 9
Date: April 1965

At first, it seemed appropriate to end this letter run and the book with the damning finality of the previous letter. It did damn me and I knew when I read it that I had wrecked the relationship. At the very least there was going to be a long gap and I had no faith in the 'new start on a different basis'. So I resigned myself to it being over and part of me was even self-destructively content to have wrecked it .The last thing I was expecting was another letter, but I reckoned without Iris Murdoch's inability to damn anybody for very long. It arrived three days after the first one.

Dear David,
All right, I've calmed down a bit now. I still believe what X said, but maybe you aren't as guilty as I thought at first. I imagined some kind of systematic malice and this now doesn't now seem just – though instinct can produce systems. I think you are more of a connoisseur of cruelty than you admit to being. But you are quite right that I must take responsibility for the risk involved in befriending you. (You say defensively you are 25 – most other people I know of 25 are kind and discreet.) I didn't mean I wasn't going to see you. Having taken you on as a friend I can't go back on that. I was blindingly angry with you after I received X's letter but the anger has cooled. I still need time to get over this though. I'll see you later, maybe sooner than I said.

Written along the side:
You should not keep carbon copies of personal letters

David Morgan was born in the most non- of non-places, a commuter suburb of Birmingham. After an interrupted education that included a school for maladjusted boys and King Edward VI Grammar School, Stratford-upon-Avon, he left without qualifications and spent the next six years educating himself. Getting into the Royal College of Art, where in 1964 he met Iris Murdoch, proved to him that he couldn't paint but maybe he could write and teach and, encouraged by her, he ended up running part-time studies at a London University. Like many autodidacts he has a 'quiz' knowledge of the world with many gaps but would have had many more if he hadn't met her. Incapable of concentrating and getting good at one thing, he has ducked and dived through things as wide apart as concrete poetry, dyslexia therapies and rubber sheet maths, believing, with the crankiness of the self-taught, that he could break new ground in each. The closest he has come is in the field of 3D fractals where he believes he has made genuine discoveries but can't explain them in a language a mathematician would understand. His debt to IM is that she confirmed for him he had a mind – which he had always suspected. He lives in London, has one daughter, and is continuing to teach beyond retirement age.